THE SECOND AGE OF
REPTILES

THE SECOND AGE OF
REPTILES

Striking Discoveries about the Nature of Economic and Political Species

Warm-Blooded Books
Peabody, Massachusetts

This publication is designed to provide accurate and authoritative
information in regard to the subject matter covered. It is sold with the
understanding that neither the author nor the publisher is engaged in
rendering legal, accounting, or other professional services. If legal
advice or other expert assistance is required, the services of a
competent professional person should be sought.

*From a Declaration of Principles jointly adopted by a Committee of the
American Bar association and a Committee of Publishers.*

Publisher's Cataloging-in-Publication
(Provided by Quality Books, Inc.)

Kammel, Raafat.
   The second age of reptiles : striking discoveries
about the nature of economic and political species /
Raafat Kammel. -- 1st ed.
      p .cm.
      Includes bibliographical references and index.
      ISBN: 0-9674221-0-8

1 United States—Economic Policy—1993-
      2. United States—Politics and government—1993-
      3. Economic policy—United States.   I. Title.

   HC106.92.K36 2000   338.973
                  QBI99-1789

Warm-Blooded Books
P.O. Box 2119, Peabody, MA

Visit our Web site at www.warm-bloodedbooks.com

Printed in the United States of America
10 9 8 7 6 5 4 3 2 1

This book is dedicated to the memory of early mammalian species that looked like mice and rats and appeared during the Age of Reptiles. Those little pioneers endured an era that was hostile to advanced species and friendly to primitive ones, just like what we the Independents and Reformists confront at present. Yet early mammals did not dwell on the negatives of their times. Instead, they fought courageously for survival until their descendants finally succeeded in defeating the reptiles and marking the beginning of the Age of Mammals. It is time to remember, honor and learn from those forgotten heroes, and follow their footsteps in economics and politics. Then they can rest in peace, knowing that the remarkable examples they left us will never be in vain.

Acknowledgements

This book has benefited considerably from friends and colleagues at General Electric Company, Aircraft Engine Group in Lynn, Massachusetts. I am specially thankful to Ann Mollica for her collaboration on an earlier version that was based on engine analogy. Although that version was never published, it gave me insight to write this version implementing biological analogy. I also thank David Carpenter, Steve Blegstad, Ron Rudolph, Mansour Saleki, George Wong, Phil Stec, Vic Correia, Antonio Gominho, Tom DeMarche, Bob Manning, Eric Lewis, Dan Demers, Steve Tung, Jake laughner, Jeff Channell, Seungwoo Ho, George Zhu, Jim Laflen and many other colleagues at Turbine Airfoil Center of Excellence for their valuable discussions, suggestions and comments.

Next, I am especially indebted to my editor Dr. Bryan Aubrey. He did an extraordinary effort to make this subject come alive for readers.

Above all, I want to express my appreciation to my wife Sonya for her patience during the long years of struggling through this effort, when it seemed as if it would never end. I also treasure the support and encouragement from my daughter Christina and my son Mark, and cherish their belief that Dad must write something cool and funny. If this book manages to put a smile on their faces and on the faces of other readers, that will be indeed a precious accomplishment.

If economics resembles any natural science, it is biology, which describes the myriad relationships among species, their exchange in food and territory, and their interdependence in what an economist might call the grand marketplace of life.

Lawrence Malkin (1987)

Contents

PART TWO
THE NATURE OF INTERNATIONAL TRADE SPECIES

PART THREE
The MISSING LINK BETWEEN HUMAN AND REPTILIAN SPECIES

PART FOUR
WHAT TO DO NEXT?

Preface

Origin of This Book

This book is the product of an evolving effort that took over twelve years. What I originally had in mind was to write about the similarity between *economic engines* and *physical engines*. The object was to simplify economic concepts by drawing similarities between them and the processes that ordinary people know about in car engines. I also wanted engineers and economists to start a dialog, to talk to each other and communicate new ideas. I had a dream that the book would draw the attention of economists and engineers to lay the foundation of a new discipline, *Economic Engineering*, that would blend ideas from economics and engineering.

As an engineer with many years of diversified experience in several types of engines including aircraft, automotive and power generation, I knew the physical side. But I needed to do my homework on the economic side. I did not know this homework would take so long—more than three times the amount of effort needed to finish the thesis of my master's degree in engineering. Over a period of five years, I spent many nights and weekends learning about economics in general, and about similarities between economic engines and physical engines in particular.

The results of such a long effort were encouraging. I found many interesting similarities, even more than what I originally had anticipated. Finally, I thought I was ready to harvest the fruits of my hard work.

Discovering the Biological Side of Economics

To confirm the proposed similarity between economies and engines, I thought about devoting a final chapter of my original book to cover parallels between economic and biological engines. By a biological engine, I mean the living machinery inside animals and inside our bodies that burns absorbed food and delivers the energy to keep animals alive and active. Such biological engines should have lots of things in common with both economic and physical engines.

I had to do more homework on biology this time. I labored through many books on biology to gather information about animals from the *biological engine* point of view. I discovered interesting facts. The ways animals operate their biological engines may be classified into three main types: *cold-blooded*, *hibernating* and *warm-blooded*.

Cold-blooded animals lack the biological thermostats that regulate body heat and energy. They rely on behavioral options to warm up or cool down their bodies, such as soaking in the sun when it is cold or retreating into the shade or a ground hole when it is hot. The principle of cold-bloodedness is similar to the principles of pure capitalism and free trade. These economic systems discourage government control and regulations on economy and trade. They rely instead on free behavioral options of individuals and firms. The symptoms of pure capitalist economies, in terms of fluctuations of business cycles, are similar to the symptoms of cold-bloodedness in animals, in terms of fluctuations in blood temperature and energy levels.

Hibernation is the exact opposite of cold-bloodedness when it comes to control and freedom, although hibernation is associated with cold blood temperature, too. Hibernating animals sacrifice will, freedom, choices, and even their conscious sense of living. They go into a coma and are controlled by hibernation chemicals. In return for these sacrifices, hibernating animals are rewarded by more assurance of survival. Hibernation is similar to government control of the economy. People sacrifice personal choices and freedom in order to obtain more assurance of economic survival and to minimize the hardships of business cycle fluctuations. The level of economic hibernation varies from slight hibernation of the liberal kind to regular hibernation of the socialist kind and finally deep hibernation of the communist kind. In addition to hibernation in domestic economies, hibernation exists in trade under the label of protectionism.

Warm-bloodedness is the third and most advanced way of producing heat and energy in animals. Warm-blooded animals have biological thermostats that apply the concept of automatic feedback control to keep their blood temperature at a constant level. The warm-blooded control system does not deprive animals of free will and conscious sense of living like hibernation control. Warm-bloodedness combines and exceeds the advantages of cold-bloodedness—in terms of freedom and living—and the advantages of hibernation—in terms of better survival opportunity in cold or seasonal environment. In addition, warm-bloodedness gets rid of the miserable side effects of both cold-bloodedness and hibernation.

Since warm-blooded animals have biological thermostats installed in their brains, warm-blooded economic systems should also have economic thermostats that apply the same concept of automatic feedback control. The economic thermostats must be installed in the brains of economic and political systems. These thermostats will be computer software that automate the decision-making process of the federal government in stabilizing business cycles and balancing trade. The thermostats will replace the discretionary power of government officials, including the President, Congress, and Federal Reserve Board. The economic and trade thermostats will be developed by competing firms in the private sector. When people cast their vote, they will elect business cycles and trade thermostats in addition to government officials. In fact, electing the thermostats will be more important and will attract more media coverage than electing government officials, as the latter will lose most of their discretionary power in setting economic and trade policies.

At present, there is no single economic or trade system in the entire world that we can classify as warm-blooded. All systems apply a mix of cold-bloodedness and hibernation to varying degrees. Hibernation is more of a reptilian than mammalian habit since all reptiles living in seasonal regions hibernate in winter compared to only a small fraction of mammals. Also, hibernation was practiced by reptiles long before mammals appeared. Because of the lack of warm-bloodedness in all economic and political systems and the dominance of cold-bloodedness and hibernation, we indeed live in the *Age of Reptilian Economics and Politics.*

Love and Adventure with the Biological Side of Economics

The discovery of the similarity between economic and biological systems was striking. The biological similarity suggests that Republicans and free trade proponents are cold-blooded reptiles. It also suggests that Democrats and protectionists are a hibernating species.

In no country in the entire world at present is there a single economic and political species that can be classified as warm-blooded, nothing to reach a level comparable to respectable warm-blooded species such as mice, rats, pigs and turkeys! All economic and political systems around the world are reptilian. All of them are primitive. All of them are inferior.

With these findings, I felt my eyes were suddenly opened after having been blind. I could see new things I couldn't notice before. I could see the great danger of having reptilian species control our lives and the future of our children, and I wanted to warn readers about these evil species and the danger of letting them thrive in the habitats of economics and politics. We must do something. We must exterminate these primitive reptilian species and make room for advanced warm-blooded ones.

With such new vision, I saw the biological analogy so beautiful, so attractive and so elegant. I fell in love with biology. There were many reasons to justify my love for biology. The biological analogy is more alive than the engine analogy, more dramatic and more humorous. It arouses the emotions. It has more than just the emotional side. It is also more sophisticated and more intellectual. It has everything one could want for in a loved partner.

When one falls in love, he has to show his devotion. He has to prove that he shares his love with no one else. I decided, therefore, to toss away the original book and write a new one that would be entirely dedicated to the biological analogy. What started out as a single chapter in the original book became an entire book.

Devotion is not the only thing associated with love. Cost of time, money or both is another factor. That was particularly true of my love for the biological analogy. It cost me seven more years during which I spent evenings and weekends reading about biology and economics and searching for all the similarities between them. That made the total time in which I was collecting information related to this book twelve years.

As I gathered more information on the biological side of economics, I found the material growing rapidly. It became too big to fit in a single book. I decided, therefore, to divide the material into a multi-volume series.

Parts of This Book

This volume explores the *Nature of Species* dwelling in the habitats of economics and politics. The book contains four parts that examine their nature from different angles and different applications.

The first part deals with the *nature of domestic species*. Conservatives are cold-blooded reptiles. Liberals are hibernating species. The part explains what it takes for reptilian economic and political species to cross the boundary from reptilism to warm-bloodedness.

The second part deals with the *nature of international trade species*. Free trade proponents are cold-blooded reptiles. Protectionists are hibernating species. Many trade systems apply a mix of free trade and protectionism to varying degrees. There is, at present, no single trade species that can be qualified as warm-blooded.

The third part reveals the *missing link between human and reptilian species*! This may sound more outrageous than the claims of a missing link between humans and apes. After all, reptiles are much more primitive and more inferior than apes—which makes the gap between both sides of the link so huge. To provide evidence for this link, the third part discusses the philosophy of cold-bloodedness, hibernation, and what goes on in the minds of economic and political species, showing that they are a reflection of a reptilian mentality.

The fourth and final part covers *what to do after understanding the nature of the inferior reptilian species* that currently rule the world of economics and politics. We must *declare war* against them. The war will be entirely intellectual as there will be not a single bullet fired or drop of blood shed. The fourth part explains how to build and organize the *Warm-Blooded Army*. It also provides interesting information on the strategy and tactics for the brutal fight against the reptilian enemy.

What Is the Main Purpose of This Book?

This book is basically about a controversial intellectual trial. The book accuses all current economic and political species of betraying the mammal class and embracing the reptile class. The readers of this book are the jurors of such an intellectual trial. Unlike typical criminal trials in which the number of jurors are limited to a few, this case can accommodate any number, even millions. The suspects in this trial will involve all the economic and political species in Washington, including the big names such as Bill Clinton, Denny Hastert, Alan Greenspan, and all other conservative and liberal politicians running for the year 2000 election.

The book urges readers to exercise their power to execute all suspect reptilian species with no mercy. Obviously, the execution shouldn't be physical by electrifying them in the electric chair, injecting them with a lethal chemical or throwing them into the gas chamber. We are dealing with an intellectual not a criminal trial. Therefore, we should settle for executing the suspect species intellectually by ignoring them and by seeking new warm-blooded solutions and leaders. With these possibilities, the intellectual criminal trial of the suspect reptilian species will be as controversial and puzzling as O.J. Simpson's criminal trial, if not more.

Shifting Mental Gears

Like any criminal trial, we need strong, solid evidence to convince the jurors beyond any reasonable doubt that all the current economic and political species are guilty of reptilism. The basis of all our evidence presented in this book is the similarity (or analogy) between biological species on one side and economic and political species on the other side. I will show hundreds of similarities in this book and the next volumes. In each case, I will first present some simple biological facts that the average reader will easily understand. Then I will translate such facts from biological language to economic and political language.

We will go through many translations between biological systems and economic and political systems. But don't feel overwhelmed by going through those numerous mental trips. I have a plan to make them as easy, comfortable and enjoyable as possible. It will be like shifting gears in your car.

When you drive your car, you make many gear shifts back and forth. We will do the same here in this book, but with just two gears: biology gear and economics/politics gear. An important part in driving cars is to know what the current gear is. Without such knowledge, driving would be dangerous. Auto engineers, therefore, design car consoles in such a way that the driver can determine with a quick, effortless look what gear the car is in.

I have done something similar in the design of this book so that with no effort, the reader knows whether the gear of the current information is the biology gear or the economics/politics gear. I used, therefore, two colors in printing the text material: blue and black. Every time you see text printed in blue, it means it is biological material. Materials printed in black will be related to economics and politics. Using different colors to indicate the current engaged gear should make it more vivid than explaining it with words.

The blue material will run for one or several paragraphs. Once the color changes from blue to black, it means that the biological story is over. The reader may want to take a little break for a minute or so and think about how to translate the biological facts into economic and political facts. A quick way of doing the translation is to change key words from biological to economic and political terminology. In some cases, you may keep more than 90 percent of the words unchanged. As you practice, you will find that it is much simpler than translating between English and any foreign language.

You will notice that we will start each point with the biological facts (printed in blue) that everyone agrees upon. All readers, from extreme conservatives to extreme communists, should accept the credibility of the material printed in blue. After all, these are simply biological facts supported by science. They contain no ideology or doctrine aimed at turning on the emotion and turning off the logic.

After the first gear that relies on biological facts is engaged for a while, it will be time to shift to the second gear—the translation of the biological information into economic and political terms. After the second gear is successfully engaged, we will cruise into a new, innovative understanding of economics and politics.

The process of shifting gears in this book is different from the typical style of gear engagement in economics and politics. Most discussions in those areas skip the first gear and go directly into the second gear. If you skip the first gear when driving a car, you will hurt the engine and it is likely to stall. The same thing happens in economical and political discussions which skip the gear that transmits scientific knowledge and directly engages the second gear that relies on ideology and doctrines. Like improper shifting of gears in a car, we end up hurting the soundness of the arguments and stalling the power of the conclusion.

We can avoid these disappointments with the practice of shifting the biological and economical/political gears. I invite readers to try it. The readers should have fun as they explore the secret back roads between the biological territories and the economic and political territories. They should have a serious look, however, at what they are doing. After all, the readers are the jurors of the proposed intellectual trial of the reptilian species that rule humans all over the world.

Making the Final Judgment Call

Let's hope that facts and truth finally prevail, and that you and other readers will come up with a just verdict in this intellectual trial. But no matter what most people decide, you must try your best to answer these questions:

- Are the current economic and political species guilty of betraying the mammal class and flirting with the reptile class or not guilty (by reason of insanity)?
- Will the political species running in the historical year 2000 election be different than the current reptilian ones? (Something to think about before wasting your vote on George

Bush, Al Gore, and other Republican and Democratic politicians running for the House and Senate.)

- Should these reptilian economic and political species be sentenced to a mass extinction similar to the one that wiped out their dinosaur relatives at the end of the Age of Reptiles? Or should they be allowed to continue abusing us and controlling our future and the future of our children?

Before you make your final judgment in this *intellectual trial of the new millennium* , I urge you to devote plenty of time and deep thought to the simple biological facts presented in this book. You will see that they can be logically translated into vivid economic and political facts that cry out loud for condemning and exterminating the suspect reptilian species. On the positive side, these facts will inspire us to end the *Dark Age of Reptilian Economics and Politics,* and define a new beginning for the *Enlightened Age of Mammalian Economics and Politics*, an age that will start soon and last until the end of time!

PART ONE

THE NATURE OF DOMESTIC SPECIES

1
Cold-Bloodedness and Its Misery

So, what I'd really like is a *new label*. And I'm sure there are a lot of people who feel the same. We are *Republican Party Reptiles*. We look like Republicans, and think like conservatives. [1]

P.J. O'Rourke (1987)

The *fault*, dear Brutus, is not in our stars—but *in ourselves*.

William Shakespeare,
Julius Caesar

Biologically We Belong to Warm-Blooded Species

We humans are magnificent creatures. We are intelligent, adaptive, curious and social animals. We are thirsty for knowledge and seek the answer to every question that pops into our minds. We find pleasure and satisfaction in providing the highest level of care to our children. We strive for a better world for ourselves and our descendants. With these advantages, we rose in the animal kingdom to control the planet and its future.

The human species belongs to a class of animals called mammals. This class is the highest of the five vertebrate classes that comprise the animal kingdom. A vertebrate animal is one with a backbone. The five vertebrate classes, in order of their appearance on Earth, are fish, amphibians, reptiles, mammals and birds. Compared to other classes, the entire mammal class enjoys many of the same advantages that distinguish humans. Next to mammals, the bird class has a fairly good score.

The advanced classes of mammals and birds have a common feature that is crucial to their superiority. They are warm-blooded. Warm-blooded animals maintain an ideal steady body temperature irrespective of their external environment, which may vary from extremely cold to extremely hot. Their brains are equipped with a precise thermostat called the hypothalamus. This thermostat is designed to effectively handle both excessive heat loss to a cold environment and excessive heat gain from either hot surroundings or prolonged physical activity. Because of this precise thermostat, warm-blooded animals are highly successful in all geographical regions and fully active in all climates.

Economically and Politically We Belong to Reptilian Species

Unfortunately, when it comes to living in the world of economics, humans are a primitive and miserable species. Unlike warm-blooded animals that maintain steady body temperature and high activity levels irrespective of the external environment, our economic activities, including unemployment rates, interest rates, and inflation figures fluctuate excessively. These unnecessary fluctuations qualify us to belong economically to the cold-blooded reptilian species.

And it doesn't stop there. Politics is closely related to economics. An important part of being a successful politician is to package and sell reptilian economic theories to simple-minded voters. Because of this close linkage between economics and politics it is clear that we belong to the reptilian species in both disciplines.

In order to understand our reptilian ranking in the world of economics and politics, we need to understand our closest relatives in that world. We need to know more about the miserable reptile class and all the things that their biological systems have in common with our economic and political systems.

Parallels between Reptilian Blood Temperature Cycles and Business Cycles

Reptiles are *cold-blooded* animals. This means that on a cold day their blood temperature falls and they become sluggish and move slowly. On a hot sunny day their blood temperature rises and they become more active. They lack the precise thermostats that warm-blooded mammals and birds have as a part of their brains.

Reptiles experience cycles of blood temperature and activity fluctuations. Each of these cycles can be divided into four phases: trough, expansion, peak, and recession, as shown in Figure 1. The trough happens when the external environment reaches its coldest temperature. At this point, the reptile moves at its slowest and becomes the most vulnerable. Following the trough, the expansion phase is when the environment warms up and the reptile's activity increases. The blood temperature rises, too. At the peak, the blood temperature and activity reach the highest level. Finally, recession

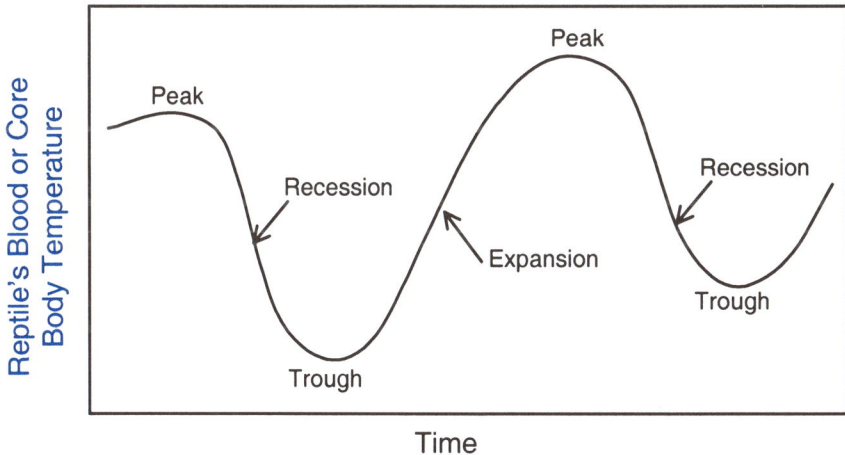

Time

Figure 1:   Four Phases of Reptile's Blood Temperature and Activity Rate Cycles

Note: This chart may be used also to represent business cycles. Just replace "Reptile's Blood Temperature" with "Inflation Rate."

occurs when the environment gets colder, and the reptile's activity decreases and its blood temperature falls. The cycle repeats itself in endless successions of ups and downs that reflect the temperature of the external environment.

Capitalist economies exhibit the same cyclical features as reptiles. They are *cold-blooded*. This means that in cold periods of recessions and depressions, inflation rates and economic activities fall. Firms move slowly. Consumers tighten their spending. During warm periods, called economic expansions and prosperity, firms and consumers become more active. Inflation rises frequently. *Cold-blooded* economies lack the economic thermostats that future *warm-blooded* economies will have as a part of the brains of their systems.

Capitalist economies experience the same four phases that reptiles exhibit in their blood temperature and activity level. Of course, the terminology is different. Blood temperature becomes inflation rate and physical activity becomes economic activity, as measured by national output, unemployment rates or economic growth. There is an additional difference. The time period for a reptilian main cycle is typically a year, with peaks in summers and troughs in winters. But the business cycle extends to several years. Also, business cycles tend to have more complex variations than reptilian cycles. Despite such minor differences, Figure 1 can be used to describe both reptilian and economic cycles. One needs only to change the label on the vertical axis, and the time values on the horizontal axis.

In both reptilian and business cycles, there are short-term cycles imposed on the main ones. For reptiles, such cycles are due to fluctuations in temperatures, days and nights. For business cycles, seasonal fluctuations create similar effects. In addition, both major cycles could be imposed on long-term cycles. Changes in climate over the years or decades will be reflected in the reptilian cycles and produce patterns similar to long-term fluctuations in business cycles.

The resemblance of business cycles to the fluctuations of the weather—that basically govern the reptilian blood temperature cycles—was acknowledged by Paul Samuelson, a Nobel Prize Winner in economics:

No exact formula, such as might apply to the motions of the moon or the pendulum, can be used to predict the timing of business cycles. Rather, in their irregularities, business cycles more closely resemble the fluctuations of the weather. [2]

The Cost of Cold-Bloodedness

Blood temperature and activity cycles impose two costs on the reptile. The first is waste—the loss of feeding and living-to-full-potential opportunity that could have been achieved had the animal been warm-blooded. The second cost is insecurity and hardship. Young and weak animals are the most vulnerable to the strike of cold weather.

Business cycles, too, impose similar costs on society. The first is waste—the loss of jobs, goods and services that society needed and could produce if its economy was warm-blooded. The second is the personal insecurity and hardship it creates for laid-off workers, their families and their children.

Waste is manifested in several forms. Firms run their factories at low capacity. Unemployed workers sit idle at home. Consumers cannot buy the goods and services they need. The late economist Arthur Okun developed an interesting formula to quantify such waste. This formula, known as Okun's law, states that for every one percent increase in unemployment as a result of a business cycle, there is a generated two percent drop in national product. [3]

Applying the rule of two percent loss of national product to 1992's $6,000 billion GNP, we find that the economy sacrificed about $120 billion of GNP for every one percent increase in unemployment. Most recessions show an increase in unemployment of several percentage points, and they last for more than a year. Therefore, the loss of GNP due to economic cold-bloodedness—that a single generation would see in a few recessions—can easily accumulate to trillions of dollars.

Economic cold-bloodedness is much more than the loss of trillions of dollars; it results in mental, social and family catastrophe as well. Workers who lose their pay-checks as a result of business cycles are not the only ones to suffer. Other workers worry that they might be the ones to be laid off the next time. Many feel insecure and become demoralized. They have good reasons for such negative feelings. Being laid-off is a heavy blow to a person's feeling of worth. It indicates that he or she is not needed, cannot support a family, and is not really a full and valuable member of society. Some researchers link the psychological tension as a result of job loss and insecurity to the increase in suicides, homicides, cardiovascular mortality and mental illness. [4]

Some victims of business cycles—especially those who suffer prolonged unemployment—try to escape the tension by taking drugs. Others express their anger against society by violence, riots and joining gangs. These are social diseases that torture our society and our economy.

Families and children also pay a huge price for business cycles. We know that each time unemployment increases, there will be more battered wives, more family breakdowns and more child abuse. Indeed, innocent children are the most victimized as their education, health and security may be ruined. The damage they suffer is not repairable.

With all these tragic side effects, cold-bloodedness is as devastating for economies as it is for reptiles. Not only does it create misery for humans and reptiles, but it shows how much the two species have in common!

Why are Reptiles Hit the Hardest by Cold-Bloodedness?

Reptiles are not the only vertebrates classified as cold-blooded because their body temperature fluctuations reflect their surroundings. Fish and amphibians are also cold-blooded. Compared to the latter two vertebrate classes, reptiles are the most recent in evolution history, and therefore, the most advanced cold-blooded class. But in spite of their relatively high ranking among cold-blooded animals, reptiles are hit the hardest by cold-bloodedness. They experience higher swings in blood temperatures and activity levels relative to amphibians and fish. That makes reptiles the best example to explain the worst consequences of cold-bloodedness.

The reason for the more pronounced cycle of blood temperature and activity of reptiles is the environment in which they dwell. Reptiles are the first vertebrate animals classified as fully terrestrial. The environment they live in has higher fluctuations in temperature than water and swamps where fish and amphibians live. The aqueous environment takes longer to warm up or cool down, and therefore maintains narrower temperature fluctuations than the terrestrial environment. The tragic mass extinction of dinosaurs demonstrates that the terrestrial environment is more hostile and less forgiving to cold-bloodedness for reptiles than the aqueous environment to fish and the combined aqueous-terrestrial one to amphibians.

Capitalist economies and their political environment have several similarities to reptiles and their terrestrial environment. They are the most recent cold-blooded economies in the history of the world. Not the first, but the worst in terms of suffering from symptoms of cold-bloodedness—namely business cycles.

The first cold-blooded economic system was in ancient times. It was slave-based, associated with self-sufficient agricultural communities and political autocracy. That age is analogous to the Age of Fish—the first vertebrate class. The second system was the feudalism of the Middle Ages. This system provided limited exposure to economic and political freedom in the same way the amphibian class provided limited exposure to the terrestrial environment, but on a lower scale. The third and last cold-blooded economic system is modern capitalism. The capitalist system provided as much exposure to economic and political freedom as the reptile class had for full terrestrial living. Because they permit maximum exploration of the new environment of freedom, capitalist economies are the most advanced cold-blooded economic systems.

Despite being most recent and advanced, capitalist economies are hit the hardest by the principle characteristic of a cold-blooded economy—namely business cycles. Upward and downward swings have characterized all the capitalistic nations of the world for the last two centuries in a pattern that was never experienced in the ancient slave systems or the feudalism of the Middle Ages. That makes capitalist economies the best examples of the horrible consequences of cold-bloodedness.

The reason for the more cold-blooded nature of modern capitalism is the environment of full political and economic freedom in which we dwell. The new environment provides as many fluctuations and personal choices as the terrestrial environments provide in temperature fluctuations.

Just as the terrestrial environment offers wonderful opportunities to warm-blooded animals, so too does the freedom environment to future warm-blooded economic systems. However, they also impose huge risks to reptiles and reptilian economic systems. Without warning, they may suddenly become hostile and less forgiving to cold-bloodedness in biological or economic forms. The result can be mass extinction. It happened to dinosaurs. It will happen again to our cold-blooded reptilian economic system.

The Cold-Blooded Dilemma

The blood temperature of a reptile is not only at the mercy of external surroundings; it is also threatened by internal heat generated in its own body from physical activities. Reptiles lack the temperature control devices that help warm-blooded mammals and birds dispose of excess heat efficiently. The reptile body absorbs a large portion of the heat, thus raising its blood temperature above a comfortable level. A reptile, therefore, suffers from a temporary fever every time it is forced to perform prolonged strenuous activities.

The variation of a reptile's blood temperature in correspondence with its inactivity rate is shown in Figure 2. Note that low inactivity rate means vigor and high inactivity rate means idleness. The main reason for selecting such weird notation is that reptiles—and related economic systems—prefer idleness to vigor. The curve shows a negative correlation. This means more of blood temperature or inactivity rate is associated with less of the other. The reptilian curve is in contrast with the warm-blooded curve that forms a horizontal relationship at a fixed precise temperature.

Thus reptiles face a cruel, cold-blooded dilemma, even in an ideal environment of steady, warm temperatures all year around. If the reptile wants to avoid the discomfort resulting from an increase in blood temperature associated with prolonged activities, it has to settle for idleness. If the reptile wants to be more active, it has to endure fever, which will force it to become inactive after a little while. Reptiles are aware of this dilemma and of their energy and

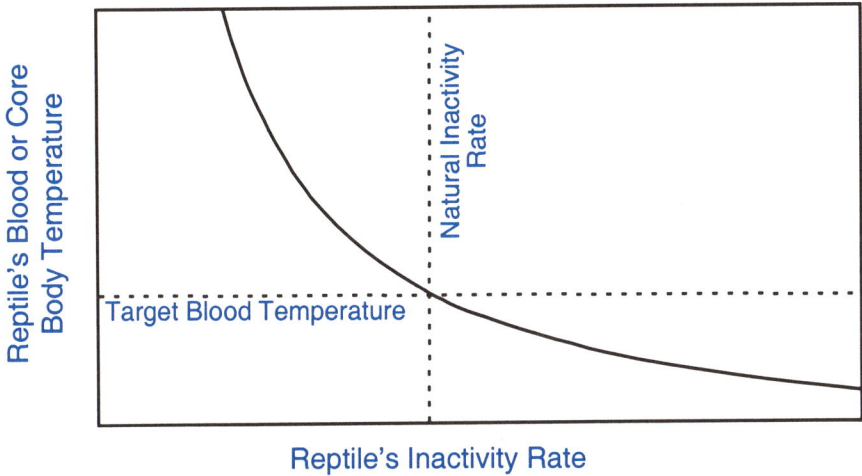

Figure 2: Relationship between Reptile's Blood Temperature and Inactivity Rate

Note: This chart may be also used to represent the behavior of a capitalist economy. It is called Phillips curve. You need to replace "Reptile's Blood Temperature" with "Inflation Rate", "Inactivity Rate" with "Unemployment Rate", "Target Blood Temperature" with "Target Inflation Rate", and "Natural Inactivity Rate" with "Natural Unemployment Rate."

blood temperature handicaps. Therefore, they prefer to stay motionless most of the time. On a few occasions, reptiles can strike on their prey quickly, but such bursts of activity are short-lived, lasting only a few seconds.

The relationship between a reptile's blood temperature and inactivity rate shown in Figure 2 is not fixed all the time. A reptile's blood temperature depends on the external temperature as well. Therefore, the curve may shift up or down, depending on the fluctuations in the temperature of the environment. A correction to account for this shift is needed in order to accurately predict the reptile's blood temperature at a given inactivity rate and a given external temperature for a given species.

The combination of ideal blood temperature and high activity rate can never be achieved in any reptilian system as Figure 2 indicates. For this, a completely different design is necessary: the warm-blooded temperature and energy control system of mammals and birds. Without such a robust control system, animals can never escape from the cold-blooded dilemma.

Capitalist economies also suffer from the same cruel dilemma. To better understand this, I invite you to do a little exercise. Go back to the beginning of this section and for all the paragraphs printed in blue change the terminology from biological systems to economic systems. This means replacing blood temperature with inflation rate and inactivity rate with unemployment rate. If you feel like rephrasing, adding or deleting other words and sentences, please do so. Also, don't forget to adjust labels on Figure 2. Then, compare your translation from reptilian systems to economic systems with mine. Armed with this tool, you will be amazed at how you can independently predict some of the most interesting ideas in macroeconomics, even if you have never taken a single course in the subject. You will have more of a real feeling for it than many of those who pay a fortune to enroll in typical classes. Most important, the proposed method of acquiring new knowledge by analogy, guessing and translation is fun.

Now it is time for me to show my own reptilian-economic translation. The inflation rate of a capitalist economy is not only at the mercy of external factors such as oil and technology shocks; it is also threatened by heat generated from its own economic activities. Capitalist economies lack economic thermostats that will help future warm-blooded economies to dispose of excess inflation heat effectively. A capitalist economy, therefore, absorbs a big chunk of the heat from economic activity and this results in raising the inflation rate above a comfortable level. Thus, a capitalist economy suffers from an inflation fever every time it is allowed to expand strenuously for a long time.

I hope you have already made the proper label changes in Figure 2 from reptilian to economic notations on both the horizontal and vertical axes. Now, you will have a modest reward for your effort. You have independently constructed what economists call the Phillips curve. You have discovered the variation of inflation rate against unemployment rate for a capitalist economy. Although the reptilian curve has been known for hundreds of years, the economic curve was discovered only in 1958 by A.W. Phillips of the London School of Economics.[5] This gives an idea about how things crawl slowly in economics.

The Phillips curve shows a negative correlation. This means more inflation, or a higher unemployment rate, is associated with less of the other. The Phillips curve is in contrast with the warm-blooded curve of future economies that will have a close to horizontal relationship at a target inflation rate. There is no single economy yet in the entire world that satisfies such warm-blooded criteria.

Figure 2 shows the capitalist dilemma, even in an ideal environment of no supply shocks. If policy makers want to avoid the discomfort resulting from inflation associated with prolonged economic activities, they have to settle for running the economy at slow speeds. If more economic activities are desired, the economy has to endure an inflation fever which will have damaging effects on personal savings and quickly force the economy into a severe recession. The Federal Reserve Board is aware of this cold-blooded reptilian dilemma. It also recognizes the handicaps of the U.S. economy when it comes to choosing between full employment and low inflation. The Fed knows the horrible consequences of high economic activity in reptilian economic systems. Therefore, the Fed feels more comfortable with cold-bloodedness—that is, running the economy at crawling speeds!

The relationship between inflation and unemployment rate shown in modified Figure 2 is not fixed all the time. There are other external factors that affect prices and inflation. Violent swings in oil prices are a good example. Interest rates affect capital cost of goods and services and how firms set prices to make profits. Global economic competition puts pressure on producers to keep costs low. Currency rates affect the cost of imports and raw materials. Internet advancements, computer-ization and productivity improvements reduce product costs. Declining union membership as a percentage of the workforce weakens the bargaining power of workers and reduces the labor costs. These are just a few examples in a long list of factors.

Each of these factors shifts the Phillips curve either up or down depending on whether the factor increases or decreases the cost of producing goods and services. As the reader may expect, some factors may have a larger influence on the final shift than others. In addition, it is very likely that some factors will be pulling the curve opposite to others. Therefore, the external factors influencing the shift of Phillips curve are more numerous and more complex than the single factor of environment temperature that governs the shift of the reptilian curve. Such complexity makes economic cold-bloodedness more erratic and more torturous than reptilian cold-bloodedness!

The combination of ideal inflation rate and high economic activity can never be achieved in any capitalist economy, as the Phillips curve indicates. This combination needs a completely different design: the warm-blooded inflation and economic activity control system of future economies. Without the new system—that requires understanding and learning from warm-blooded mammals and birds—humans can never escape from the economic version of the cold-blooded dilemma.

Power Ratings of Cold-Blooded Reptiles

Reptiles can never resolve their cold-blooded dilemma; they have to endure its misery every single day. In order to cope, reptiles must set a limit called the natural inactivity rate. Each species chooses a target for the maximum blood temperature it can tolerate. The more cold-blooded the species, the lower its blood temperature target. This target is represented by a horizontal line on the curve of blood temperature versus inactivity rate as shown in Figure 2. The inactivity rate corresponding to the intersection of the horizontal line with the curve establishes the reptile's natural inactivity rate. This rate represents the safe limit on physical activity that the reptile can sustain steadily without igniting a fever in its own body. The rate of output energy—in either watt or tiny decimal fraction of horsepower units—the reptile can deliver at such a limit is called potential output power. Reptiles live within their inferior limits of activity and potential output power.

This also holds true in our reptilian economies. One just needs to translate the biological information: replace natural inactivity rate with natural unemployment rate, and potential output power with potential economic output.

Capitalist economies can never resolve their cold-blooded dilemma of having to choose between inflation and unemployment. They must endure its misery. In order to mitigate the adverse effects, economists set a limit called the natural unemployment rate. Each society chooses a target for the maximum inflation rate it tolerates. The more cruel and cold-blooded the society and its central bank are to the workforce, the lower the inflation target. This target is represented by a horizontal line on the inflation versus unemployment rate as shown in Figure 2. The unemployment rate corresponding to the intersection of the horizontal line with the Phillips curve establishes the natural unemployment rate. This rate represents the limit on activity that the economy can sustain steadily without igniting an inflation fever. The rate of output the economy can deliver at such a limit is called potential output. Policy makers live within the economy's inferior limits of natural unemployment rate and potential output.

During the 1950s and 1960s, a common definition of natural unemployment rate was four percent. During the 1980s and early 1990s, economists believed that a figure of five or six percent was more realistic. The upward drift in natural unemployment invited an unwelcome companion: the downward trend in the growth of national output and what people expect from the economy. These have been the most disturbing trends in economic cold-bloodedness during the last three decades.

Economists came up with several explanations for the disappointing trends. The first is the rising participation of women and minorities in the labor force. These groups tend to hold less on their jobs. The second explanation blames humanitarian government policy, such as unemployment insurance, welfare and food stamps that reduce the incentive of unemployed people to look hard for jobs. These explanations bring some comfort to many of us, especially conservative white males. The fault, however, is not in women or minorities or in providing safety nets to victims of business cycles. *The fault is in the cold-blooded nature of our reptilian economic and political system!*

2
Hibernation and Sacrificing Living for Survival

It is better that we *live* so miserably than *die* in glory.
Euripides, Greek Dramatist (405 BC)

They that can give up essential liberty to obtain a little temporary *safety* deserve neither liberty nor safety.
Benjamin Franklin (1759)

Live Free or *Die*.
Quotation on car license plates of State of New Hampshire

The Need for Hibernation

As reptiles became the first fully terrestrial animals, they discovered tremendous opportunities on land: a variety of new food sources, more light, more beautiful views of landscapes with vivid colors and more oxygen to breathe. They explored new ways of locomotion including running, climbing and jumping from cliffs. They must have looked at themselves and felt satisfied and proud. They had good reason. They launched a brand new vertebrate class called class reptilia that would revolutionize the history of life. They took the risk of exploring the new terrestrial environment. Their courage and determination had finally paid off.

However, opportunity was not the only thing awaiting reptiles on their adventure on land. They faced serious problems as well. The terrestrial environment had excessive swings in temperature and food sources. There were good times, with tropical climates, lush vegetation and abundant prey. However, there were also bad times when temperatures became too cold and food scarce. Reptiles found out the hard way that they were more vulnerable to hostile environments than their amphibian and fish ancestors. The suffering and death tolls were overwhelming. But small and weaker species discovered an effective way to cope with the harsh environment and increase the chances of their survival. It was called hibernation.

Humans had similar experiences in the economic and political realm. During the late eighteenth and early nineteenth centuries, Western European nations deserted their earlier economic and political systems that were based on mercantilism and autocracy to evolve into modern capitalism and representative governments. They created the first free economic and political systems. Under these systems, there were tremendous opportunities. People enjoyed free speech, a free press, free assembly and free elections. The Industrial Revolution provided new variety in goods and jobs. Economic growth was accelerating. The invention of railroad and steamboats provided new, faster ways of locomotion. People felt proud of what they had accomplished. They had good reason. They had invented a brand new class called the *economic and political version of class reptilia* that would revolutionize the history of mankind. They had taken the risk of creating a new, free environment. Their courage and determination had finally paid off.

But with the new opportunities came horrifying problems. The economic environment had excessive swings in what are called business cycles. There were good times when there were plenty of jobs, expansion and prosperity. But there were also bad times of fewer jobs, recessions and depressions. Economists found out that capitalism was more vulnerable to the swings in the environment than the earlier economic systems of slavery and feudalism. The suffering of workers was overwhelming. But small and weaker elements in society discovered an effective way to cope with the harsh environment and increase their chances of survival. It was called economic and political hibernation and it came in three forms: communism, socialism and liberalism.

The Hibernation Deal

Hibernation is like any business deal. One pays a price and receives merchandise, a pay-off, in return. The price for animal hibernation is loss of joy of living and freedom of choices and the acceptance of coma. The pay-off lies in avoiding the torture of the freezing environment and so increasing the chance of survival.

Economic and political hibernation offers the same deal. Society pays a price and receives merchandise in return. The price for human hibernation is loss of economic, political and personal freedom. The merchandise is the avoidance or minimization of the hardship of business cycles and consequent increase in the chance of financial survival for the disadvantaged and working classes.

Symptoms of Hibernation

Hibernating animals have several common symptoms. They get cooler till their bodies are only a few degrees warmer than the air in their dens. Small hibernators become so stiff that they can be rolled about like balls. The heartbeats drop to only several beats a minute instead of 100 or 200 beats. Breathing becomes very slow and hardly noticeable. Metabolic rate is reduced by as much as 95% from its normal rate. The animal becomes unconscious and completely inactive.

The intensity of hibernation symptoms vary from one species to the other. In general, hibernators are classified into three groups: deep hibernators, average hibernators and drowsy hibernators. Deep hibernators fall into a state of apparent death with the lowest possible levels of body temperature, breathing, heartbeat and metabolism. Average hibernators have slightly higher levels of these biological functions as the animals settle for just a moderate coma. Drowsy hibernators get in a state closer to sleep than coma.

Humans suffer from the same symptoms, but expressed in economic and political terms. The most vivid example is the communist system. Under communism, private ownership for profit is either prohibited or discouraged. Instead, the state owns the means of production, sets wages and most prices, and directs the economy. The economy becomes stiff and its activity gets cold because it is centrally planned by the state. People are provided with just their simplest needs that barely keep them alive. Communism permits only a little of a person's life to remain outside the control of the party and the state. People are allowed to hear what the Communist Party wants them to know through the state-controlled media. Given these symptoms, communism is diagnosed as deep economic and political hibernation.

The second level of human hibernation is democratic socialism. Under this system, private ownership for profit is mostly permitted. Only selected key elements of the economy—such as banks, transportation and energy industries—are publicly owned. The state is expected to expand welfare and entitlement programs, and plan the economy. The government intervenes in income redistribution through highly progressive income tax. Personal freedom in all forms is allowed. Because it occupies the middle ground between deep hibernation and cold-bloodedness, democratic socialism is classified as moderate hibernation.

The third and lowest level of human hibernation is liberalism as practiced in the U.S. by Democrats. There is no restriction on private ownership. The government operates only the postal service. Intervention of government in the economy is lower compared to socialism. Still, liberals prefer the welfare state, the expansion of entitlement programs and excessively progressive income tax. Because these hibernation symptoms are slight, liberalism is classified as drowsy hibernation.

Is Hibernation a Backward Move?

When some amphibians deserted their aqueous-terrestrial environment to migrate into a fully terrestrial environment and evolve into reptiles, they were seeking more favorable opportunities. They were looking for the maximum amount of oxygen, more light, faster means of locomotion and new food sources. Because of the hostility of the terrestrial environment, some of the little species were forced into hibernation. For these species, hibernation meant giving up most of the advantages they were looking for in a terrestrial environment. It meant less breathing, less oxygen, living in darker dens, being squeezed into tiny ground holes, less locomotion and minimal or no food. Thus, reptiles living in deep hibernation did not really enjoy living more than their amphibian and fish ancestors that did not need to hibernate. Terrestrial hibernation seemed like a backward move.

Humans, too, had similar feelings about economic and political hibernation. Because of the hostility of the new economic and political environment, some of the working and lower income classes were attracted to hibernation in the form of communism, socialism or liberalism. For those classes, hibernation meant giving up some or even most of the freedom gained in the new environment. In deep communist hibernation, living was not significantly better than under slavery or feudalism. Economic and political hibernation seemed like a retreat from the environment of freedom.

Seasonal and Permanent Hibernation

Hibernators, in general, are classified according to the duration of hibernation into two categories: seasonal and permanent. The first hibernate only as necessary during the cold season. The second hibernate continuously every single day of the year regardless of whether the external environment is freezing, seasonal or even tropical! All hibernating animals—both living and extinct—fall into the category of seasonal hibernators. Permanent hibernators are found only in the economic and political systems of the human species!

There is a good reason for such a major difference. Animals must make proper hibernation decisions, otherwise their species face extinction. Only human hibernators can live indefinitely with foolish decisions in their economic and political systems!

Permanent hibernation is clearly demonstrated in communist economic and political systems. Communist parties enforce continuous, deep hibernation on people using totalitarian means. While socialist and liberal hibernators are also permanent hibernators, the democratic system does not give them a chance to enforce their views very long. If the economic climate becomes warmer or people get bored with liberal hibernation, the voters can replace socialist or liberal hibernators with conservatives—the human version of non-hibernating cold-blooded reptiles.

Everyone must appreciate democracy. It allows society to alternate between hibernating status and typical cold-blooded reptilian status. Without democracy, the economic and political system would be locked into a permanent hibernating or permanent cold-blooded reptilian position. This flexibility allows our economic and political systems to match the reptilian biological systems that can switch easily and successfully from hibernation to typical cold-bloodedness and back again. There is a major difference though. Reptiles can switch any time as needed. Humans have to wait for the election day. On many occasions, waiting can be long, torturous and even catastrophic.

Is Hibernation More Reptilian or Mammalian?

Both reptiles and mammals participate in hibernation with varying degrees and varying intensity. When most people talk about hibernation, they give examples of mammals—bears, ground squirrels, chipmunks, hamsters, hedgehogs and marmots. The truth, however, is that hibernation is more of a reptilian than mammalian habit. There are several reasons supporting this fact. First, reptiles are tropical animals; without hibernation no single species can survive in seasonal regions. This means all reptiles that live in cold climates hibernate, compared to only a small fraction of mammals. Second, the majority of hibernating reptiles fall in the category of deep hibernators. Fewer mammals—mostly of tiny sizes—reach such status. Also, hibernation was practiced by reptiles before mammals appeared.

The case for economic hibernation is easier to settle than animal hibernation. Economic hibernation—up to the present time—is entirely reptilian. All economic hibernators fall into the category of permanent hibernators, which are more primitive and rigid than seasonal ones. Primitivism and rigidity are traits of reptiles.

The fact that hibernation still persists for a few warm-blooded animals suggests that economic hibernation may persist even after many new warm-blooded economies evolve. We will witness a struggle between economic hibernation and economic warm-bloodedness for some time. The latter will eventually prevail because humans are not hibernators by nature. They are biologically true warm-blooded mammals. If they deviate from such status in their economic and political systems, the deviation will not last long.

Pre-Reptilian Hibernation

Although hibernation reaches its peak—both in participation and intensity—among species of the reptile class, its roots extended to earlier fish, amphibians and invertebrate animals. Frogs and salamanders are examples of hibernating amphibians. Some fish species, such as carp, flounder and wide-mouthed toadfish, bury themselves in mud at the bottom of the ocean and remain torpid for lengthy periods.

In the same way, economic hibernation, which reached its peak in theory during the nineteenth century and in practice during the twentieth century, had many precursors. The idea of a society in which property would be held in common and the necessities of life shared by members of the community had its roots in the earlier feudal and slave-based economic systems. In the fourth century B.C., the ancient Greek philosopher Plato proposed communal ideas in his book *The Republic*. Some of the early Christian groups held property in common during the period of brutal persecution. In the Middle Ages, Sir Thomas Moore advocated communist ideas in his book *Utopia* (1516) and similar ideas were espoused by religious groups such as Anabaptists in central Europe.

Are Bears True Hibernators?

Scientists disagree about whether a bear's winter sleep is true hibernation. Many of them do not classify bears as true hibernators because a bear's body temperature falls only several degrees during dormancy. They point out that on warm winter days, male bears prowl through the woods and find food. The females wake periodically to care for their young and nurse them. Both males and females are easily aroused from their winter sleep and warm up quickly. A deep hibernator, in contrast, may die if it is awakened too fast. In spite of such evidence, some scientists argue that bears are true hibernators. A reasonable compromise would suggest that the long sleep of bears is indeed a kind of hibernation. Yet it is not true hibernation, which leaves the body cold and rigid.

Like scientists disagreeing about whether bears hibernate, political and economic analysts and commentators disagree about whether liberal hibernation is true economic and political hibernation. Many of them do not classify liberals and Democrats as true hibernators. They point out that the hibernation symptoms of liberals—measured in loss of political and economic freedom resulting from big government—are slight compared to the true hibernators of the socialist and communist kind. Some commentators, however, argue that liberals are true hibernators. A reasonable compromise would suggest that although liberalism is a kind of economic and political hibernation, it is not true hibernation that leaves the economy and personal freedom cold and rigid.

But liberals should not cheer too much about the similarity between their drowsy pattern of economic and political hibernation and the biological hibernation of bears. They should be aware of the major differences. For more than half the year, bears behave like respectable true warm-blooded animals. Liberals never reach that status even for a minute. On the contrary, they are permanent hibernators—a characteristic that is inferior to the seasonal hibernation of reptiles. There is hope, however, that some species of liberals will evolve into a mix of drowsy hibernation and warm-bloodedness like black and brown bears. They can even go one step further and become true warm-blooded animals like polar bears that never hibernate and survive in spite of their freezing environment.

When Is Hibernation Turned On and Off?

Scientists have been puzzling over the nature and cause of hibernation for a long time. Scientific research has found evidence that hibernators have an annual clock that governs the onset and termination of the hibernation process. This clock is not very precise, however, and animals kept under constant temperature and light conditions in laboratories for several years may eventually become out-of-phase with their natural winter and hibernate in spring or summer. If the animal's clock is to operate successfully under natural conditions, it must be synchronized with natural winter.

Political analysts and thinkers, too, have been puzzling over the nature and cause of economic and political hibernation. The evidence suggests that the political sentiment of the voters in Western economies has a sort of a clock which governs the onset and termination of the economic and political hibernation process. Unlike the animal's clock that triggers hibernation every year, the voters' clock triggers a major hibernation session every six to eight decades. This cycle is as long as a person's entire life span.

The last time the voters' clock said it was time for a major liberal hibernation episode was during the ice age of the Great Depression. The horrifying casualties of the economic slump proved how vulnerable cold-blooded conservatism was to unexpected changes in climate. Liberal hibernation, therefore, made more sense, especially to threatened groups and individuals. There were many of them. As a result, liberals gained control of the presidency and both Houses of Congress for twenty consecutive years from 1932 to 1952. Even after the economic climate warmed up during the next two decades, popular liberal movements continued to expand the size and scope of the government irrespective of who won the presidency. The liberal hibernation reached its peak in President Johnson's Great Society programs of the 1960s.

Then, after more than four decades of liberal hibernation, it was time for the voters' clock to send a signal to reverse the trend and switch back to conservative cold-bloodedness. This happened in the 1980s with deregulation of the economy, banks and financial markets in the Reagan Revolution. Under the Reagan and Bush administrations, conservatism wanted to evolve into more cold-blooded reptilian forms, but a hibernating liberal Congress resisted the transformation. Had it not been for the freezing ice age of the 1990-1992 recession, President Bush could have won the 1992 election. Once the economic climate showed signs of warming up, voters turned their back on liberals and elected a conservative House and Senate in 1994. President Clinton understood the voters' sentiment in the 1996 election, displaying more signs of conservative cold-bloodedness and less of liberal hibernation than any Democratic president in history. He even sounded more cold-blooded than some moderate Republican Presidents such as Eisenhower and Nixon.

Nobody can tell for sure how long the popularity of the current conservative cold-bloodedness will last, since the clock of the voters' sentiment is less accurate than that of hibernating animals. In a few instances, the voters' clock could become out-of-phase with the economic environment and trigger liberal hibernation or conservative cold-bloodedness when the economic environment actually needs the opposite. A big surprise could come any time since the voters' clock has a mind of its own. It is a pity that the lives and future of millions of people are determined by such a peculiar clock.

How Is Hibernation Induced?

It has been reported that an extract from the blood of an animal going through a hibernation session will induce hibernation when injected into an active potential hibernator. This indicates that the factor which produces hibernation is blood-borne. A blood substance called Hibernation Induction Trigger (HIT) is thought to *hit* the biological system of a hibernator, causing it to sleep. The stronger the concentration of the substance, the deeper the level of hibernation. The animal's annual clock determines when such a substance is to be released to initiate the hibernation session and when it should be extracted from the bloodstream to terminate the session.

It has been also reported that an extract from hibernating economic systems will induce hibernation when injected into another economy. This extract is called size and economic rule of the government. Excessive regulations and taxation *hit* economic activities, causing them to fall asleep the same way that HIT does for hibernating animals. The stronger the concentration of the substance, the deeper is the level of economic hibernation. The voters' clock determines when such a substance is to be released to initiate economic hibernation and when it should be extracted from the bloodstream of the economy to terminate it.

There is leaking information that many of the advocates of economic hibernation, whether liberals, socialists or communists, may have their own bodies too contaminated with the Hibernation Induction Trigger substance! The argument is that economic and biological hibernation are interrelated; they cannot be safely isolated. Some researchers speculate that if a significant amount of HIT is extracted from the blood of human hibernators and injected into a potential hibernating animal, it will cause it to sleep, even in summer. Others propose periodic monitoring of blood samples from politicians and key economists for possible contamination with HIT!

In the name of scientific research, any person who holds key information about the concentration of HIT in blood samples of human hibernators must speak·up. Such information is critical as it would strengthen the analogy between economic and biological systems presented in this book series.

Hibernation and Primates

The great majority of primates—such as the species of baboons, orangutans, gorillas and chimpanzees—never hibernate. There is one group that violates this trend. It is at the bottom of the primates' family tree, and includes the fat-tailed and mouse lemurs. These animals estivate. Estivation is similar to hibernation and is needed in desert regions when a few animals escape the hot, dry season by entering a torpid state.

In addition to the species at the bottom of the order primates, there is another species at the top that also violates the non-hibernating trend. It is the human species! Many of them, as we have seen, practice hibernation in their economic and political systems. It is ironic that humans, who have the most superior biological systems and the best brains of all primates, do things that foolish.

Biologists are urged to rethink the classification of animals in the primates' family tree. Biologists call such family tree order primates. They should kick out the fat-tailed and mouse lemurs and any other hibernating or estivating animals from the order primates. There should not be any excuse about how little the animal, or how harsh the environment, and whether the species has other impressive credentials. Biologists must recognize that from now on they have to assume economic and political responsibilities in addition to their scientific duties! They should avoid narrow tunnel vision, looking at things only from a purely biological point of view.

As biologists reclassify the order primates and make sure that it is free from all forms of animal hibernation, humans will find out that they are the only violator of the non-hibernating trend in order primates. They will be ashamed of themselves as they discover that there is no other primate that shares hibernation misery with them. That should create more incentives for humans to *confront their hibernation behavior in economic and political systems and do something about it!*

3
Hard Choices

The *choice of a point of view* is the initial act of a culture.

José Ortega y Gasset (1923)

Nobody can honestly think of himself as a strong character because, however successful he may be, he is necessarily aware of the *doubts and temptations that accompany every important choice.*

W. H. Auden (1964)

Important Choice in Biology, Economics and Politics

During the Age of Reptiles, each species had to make a critical decision about which kind of body energy and blood temperature system most suited its needs, size, lifestyle and environment. Such a decision involves choosing between *free behavior* associated with pure cold-bloodedness and *command behavior* associated with deep hibernation. That important decision affected every single characteristic of the animal's lifestyle.

Humans faced a similar situation. During the last two centuries, each society had to make a critical decision about which kind of economic system to adopt. This involved choosing between *free behavior* associated with cold-blooded capitalism versus *command behavior* associated with hibernating communism or socialism. That decision affected every single characteristic of the society, such as job creation, unemployment rates, growth, technological advances, adaptation to changing environment, ranking, competitive advantage, and most important, probability of future survival or extinction of the economic system.

The Choice of Pure Cold-Bloodedness

At the extreme right of the biological spectrum, a large population of the reptilian dynasty adopted pure cold-bloodedness. The design philosophy of such a biological system relied entirely on the animal's free behavior options to regulate its blood temperature and energy levels. Examples of these discretionary options include soaking the body in the sun if it's too cold, retreating into a cave or a ground hole if it's too hot, or any possible combination depending on the luck of finding a favorable external source. This design needs no blood temperature and energy regulatory system.

The main rationale for pure cold-bloodedness is that freedom of choice for animals is valued the most and free behavior options are adequate for regulating blood temperature. If cold-blooded reptiles were given a chance to brag about their inferior biological systems, they would argue that their freedom is likely to be undermined by blood temperature control systems that may be either of the hibernating or warm-blooded kinds. Any blood temperature control system, therefore, is deemed unnecessary, if not harmful. In this view, the reptile's blood temperature is naturally stable at desirable levels. Even when blood temperature and the ability to perform physical activity fluctuate, the fluctuations are natural, an optimal response to a changing external environment. Advocates of cold-bloodedness would claim that a biological control system should not stabilize blood temperature and body energy, even if it were possible. Their slogan would be: *"The biological system that governs blood temperature and body energy the least governs the best!"*

The extreme right of the economic and political spectrum witnessed something similar. Some societies adopted the economic version of pure cold-bloodedness. This version had non-biological labels such as *pure capitalism, classical capitalism, laissez-faire* and *libertarianism*. The design philosophy of these economic systems relied entirely on free behavior options of firms and individuals to regulate economic activities. The success of these options depends on the luck of finding a favorable external condition. This design needs no government control on the economy. Nineteenth-century America came as close as any economy to being purely cold-blooded. Such a system is admired by Republicans and conservative economists, especially those of the University of Chicago. In praising this system, the famous Nobel-prize winner, Milton Friedman, wrote:

> The combination of economic and political freedom produced a golden age in both Great Britain and the United States in the nineteenth century. [1]

The main rationale for the design philosophy of cold-blooded capitalism is that freedom of choice for firms and individuals is valued the most and free behavior options are adequate for regulating the economy and meeting society's desired ends. The proponents of this system argue that freedom is likely to be undermined by government control of the economy. Any government control, therefore, is deemed unnecessary, if not harmful. In this view, the economy is self-regulating and is naturally stable at ideal levels. According to real-business-cycle theory, economic fluctuations are natural, an optimal response to changes in the environment just as the fluctuations of reptiles' blood temperature are a natural response to changes in seasons! Advocates of cold-blooded capitalism argue that government should not stabilize the economy, even if it were possible. They proclaim that, *"Government that governs the economy the least governs the best."*

The Choice of Deep Hibernation

At the extreme left of the biological spectrum, another new design philosophy, deep hibernation, appeared to challenge cold-bloodedness. It relied entirely on the command mode instead of the free behavior mode and eliminated behavioral options. This design needs a hibernation control system to govern most, if not, all biological functions once the animal enters the hibernation coma.

The rationale for hibernation is that typical reptilian cold-bloodedness cannot provide adequate survival opportunity for small and vulnerable species caught in harsh, cold climates. During Ice Ages, many of those species face extinction. To help small species to survive, there is a need to switch from free behavior mode to command driven mode. Animals, therefore, need to give up freedom of choice and even stop living. They should be governed by a rigid code programmed in their bodies. If hibernating animals were awakened and given a chance to brag about their biological systems, they would argue that preserving life is the most important thing, that free behavioral options are inadequate to deal with an extremely cold environment. The hibernation control system, therefore, can do a great deal to overcome the limitations of cold-blooded reptilian systems.

Again, humans witnessed the same experience. At the extreme left of the economic and political spectrum, a hibernation version appeared on the horizon. It was communism, the exact opposite of laissez-faire cold-blooded capitalism. It relied mostly on the command mode that takes control over firms and individuals instead of the free behavior mode. This design needs the government to take a more active role and control most, if not, all economic functions.

The rationale for such a design philosophy is that pure capitalism cannot provide adequate survival mechanisms for workers in cold, harsh periods of the business cycle. During recessions and depressions, many workers lose their jobs and face financial ruin. To help them and their families to survive, there is a need to switch from a free economy to a command-driven economy. Firms and individuals, therefore, need to give up freedom of choice and accept being controlled by a rigid code programmed by the government. Proponents of economic hibernation argue that preserving financial survival for the working people is more important than trying to hold on to freedom of choice and living to full potential. The government control system, therefore, can do a great deal to overcome the limitations of pure capitalist economies.

The Choice of *Mix and Match*

Pure cold-bloodedness and deep hibernation defined the limits on the extreme left and extreme right of the biological design philosophy. Many reptilian species chose a variable *mix and match* of cold-bloodedness and hibernation. The mix has *two types*. The first is the *intensity mix* in which hibernation intensity is reduced from deep hibernation to either moderate or drowsy hibernation. The second type is the *seasonal mix*. This means that during the cold season, the animal abandons typical cold-bloodedness and switches to the hibernation mode. During the warm season, it abandons hibernation and switches back to typical cold-bloodedness. Such mixed designs characterized most reptilian species from the Age of Reptiles to the present.

The main rationale for the mix concept is that preserving life is as important as the combination of the animal's freedom and living to full potential. Just as pure cold-bloodedness suffers from severe limitations, so does deep hibernation. The proponents of the mixed systems saw pure cold-blooded designs ignoring the importance of preserving life and species survival. They also saw deep hibernation designs ignoring the importance of free behavior and living to full potential. There is a need, therefore, to target a balance and reasonable compromise between both extremes.

Economic and political systems had a similar experience. Many economic systems chose a variable *mix and match* of cold-bloodedness and hibernation. Such systems are called *mixed economies*. Unlike biological systems that have only *two* types of mix, economic and political systems have *three* types.

The first is the *intensity mix* in which the intensity of human hibernation is reduced from deep hibernation (communism) to either moderate hibernation (socialism) or drowsy hibernation (liberalism). Since discretionary government control of the economy is the source of economic hibernation, the intensity mix means varying the degree of government participation and control of the economy.

The second mix type is the *seasonal mix* and is achieved by democracy. This means, during cold seasons like the Great Depression, the voters may abandon conservative cold-bloodedness and switch to liberal hibernation. During warmer economic seasons, voters may choose to abandon liberal hibernation and switch back to conservative cold-bloodedness. All hibernating reptiles have this kind of flexibility in switching back and forth as needed. Thanks to democracy, we can achieve something similar, although humans tend to be more sluggish than reptiles when a change of their status is called for!

The third mix type is the *class mix* and is unique to economic and political systems. These systems deal with two major classes: the government on one side and the people and the economy on the opposite side. The status of the government, whether cold-blooded or hibernating, tends to be opposite to that of the people and the economy. For instance, in a communist system, the society and the economy fall into deep hibernation, while top-ranking officials of the communist party enjoy powerful discretionary options on regulating the economy and politics. Those government officials enjoy the same status of cold-blooded reptiles that assume full discretionary decisions in regulating blood temperature and energy levels. Hibernation of the economy, therefore, is associated with cold-bloodedness of the government.

The opposite is true for a purely capitalist economy. The government assumes a hands-off role when it comes to economic issues, as if it was hibernating. At the same time, the business cycles experience greater swings and more symptoms of cold-bloodedness. Cold-bloodedness of the economy, therefore, is associated with hibernation of the government.

In all reptilian economic systems, the higher the level of cold-bloodedness or hibernation of the government, the higher is the opposite level of the economy and society.

The class mix makes economic and political reptilism more complex and puzzling than biological reptilism. For reptiles, it is easy to figure out whether the reptile is in a cold-blooded or hibernation mode; there is only one possibility. But in economic and political systems, both kinds exist at the same time if you compare the status of the government with that of the society and the economy. Such a pattern indicates that when it comes to economics and politics, hibernation and cold-bloodedness are closer than what most people might think. It seems that the world of economics and politics is round. If you sail to the far right seeking cold-bloodedness of the economy, you will encounter hibernation (absence) in government. If you sail to the far left seeking hibernation (rigid control) over the economy and people, you will discover a hidden form of cold-bloodedness in the government.

While class mix is common for all reptilian economic systems, the term *mixed economies* is usually associated with intensity and seasonal mix types. Mixed economies try to balance cold-bloodedness and hibernation of the government on one side with that of the economy and people on the other side.

The main reason for choosing mixed economies is that stabilizing the economy and preserving the financial life of workers are important. The combination of economic and political freedom is also important. Just as pure capitalism suffers from severe limitations, so does communism. The proponents of mixed economies saw pure capitalist designs ignoring the importance of stabilizing the economy. They also saw command economies ignoring the importance of economic and political freedom. Such mixed designs have characterized all economic and political systems of Western nations and many other countries during the twentieth century.

Choice and Climate

In tropical climates, the choice of cold-bloodedness makes more sense than hibernation. In fact it would not be wise to hibernate if there is no urgent need to do so. On the other hand, the choice of hibernation makes more sense in freezing climates. It would not be wise to die in dignity, proving dedication to cold-bloodedness. Instead, it would be more practical to submit to hibernation no matter how dismaying it might be to give up the sense of living for a while.

So it is in economic and political systems. In periods of warm economic climates, the choice of cold-blooded conservatism makes more sense than hibernating liberalism, socialism or communism. In fact, it wouldn't be wise for any nation to accept any kind of hibernation coma if it can survive safely for a reasonable period of time under cold-blooded conservatism. On the other hand, the choice of economic hibernation makes more sense during freezing economic climates. When people come face to face with financial death, economic and political freedom does not mean much to them. As economic crises deepen, such as during the Great Depression, people will be more willing to accept economic and political hibernation, in the form of liberal policies.

Choice and Body Size

Large reptiles experience less fluctuations of blood temperature than small ones in the same external environment. This was confirmed by scientific studies that monitored the body temperature of crocodiles and little lizards. Crocodiles experienced smaller fluctuations of blood temperature. This indicates that body size is a key factor in minimizing the hardships of cold-bloodedness. Gigantic dinosaurs had an even larger body size than crocodiles. They were likely to have a fairly constant body temperature regardless of fluctuations in temperatures during days and nights. By contrast, small reptiles are more vulnerable to cold-bloodedness. They would have no choice but to hibernate during cold periods.

Before we explore the rule of body size effect in economics and politics, we need to see how to translate it. Body size in animals is the equivalent of financial size or net worth of humans. The rich resemble gigantic animals; the poor parallel little ones.

Just as gigantic animals experience only minor fluctuations in blood temperature, even when they are equipped with cold-blooded biological systems, the rich experience little fluctuations in their income throughout all periods of business cycles, even when the economy goes through severe recessions. Just as gigantic reptiles do not mind cold-bloodedness and do not need hibernation, the rich do not mind conservatism and do not need liberalism. Statistics confirm that conclusion. The upper classes favor the Republican Party more than the Democratic Party.

On the other hand, the fluctuations in income and job opportunities for the poor under cold-blooded capitalism is similar to the fluctuations in blood temperature of small reptiles equipped with cold-blooded biological systems. The lower and middle class, therefore, see the ugly side of cold-blooded conservatism. Because of their hardships, they are more willing to accept liberal hibernation. Statistics confirm that the lower, vulnerable classes vote more for the Democratic Party.

Choice and Gender

There are no gender differences in animals as far as cold-bloodedness and hibernation are concerned. Animals need to mate in order to preserve their species. The males and females of each species must have the same cold-bloodedness or hibernation tendency.

In contrast, humans have more flexibility in choosing between cold-bloodedness and hibernation in economics and politics. Males and females may have different views and still have a relationship. Statistics show that more males favor conservatism while more females favor liberalism. This should be expected in the light of the rule of body size effect. Males tend to be more wealthy than females. In addition, there is a difference in personality between the two sexes. A majority of males enjoy the thrills of risk-taking, exploring exciting adventures and wild roller coaster rides associated with cold-blooded conservatism. On the other hand, most females do not care so much for risky adventures. They place a higher value on the security of hibernating liberalism.

The Debate over Reptilian Choices

The debate over the issue of whether reptilian biological designs should be cold-blooded, hibernating or mixed has been going for over two hundred million years since the beginning of the Age of Reptiles. The arguments of the three sides seem plausible. Proponents of cold-bloodedness give impressive speeches about the importance of freedom of choice and living to full potential. Proponents of hibernation give equally impressive arguments about the need to preserve life and allow the survival of species. Proponents of mixed cold-bloodedness/hibernation stress the need to compromise, mix and match.

There is no simple and compelling case for the superiority of any particular view. Since the debate over the three hard choices is difficult to resolve in any way, a complete resolution of the biological controversy cannot be settled within class reptilia. The only way to find the smart final resolution is to *jump from class reptilia and seek new warm-blooded alternatives.*

Economic and political systems have a similar controversial debate about whether their designs should be laissez-faire, controlled by big governments or mixed. The debate has been going on for over two hundred years. The arguments of the three sides seem plausible. Cold-blooded conservatives can give impressive sermons about the holiness of economic and political freedom and living to full economic potential. Hibernating liberals, socialists and communists can give equally impressive sermons about the sacredness of preserving financial life and fair survival opportunity for the working class. Present-day moderates have a logical argument about the need to compromise, to mix and match between conservative cold-bloodedness and liberal hibernation.

There is no simple and compelling case that would favor any particular view of the three sides of conservatives, liberals and moderates. Since the debate over the three hard choices is difficult to resolve in any way, a complete resolution of the economic and political controversy can never be settled within our reptilian economic and political system. The only way to find the final resolution is to *jump from the economic and political version of class reptilia and seek new warm-blooded alternatives.* Once this is realized, an *extremely hard* choice becomes an *easy* one!

4

Crossing Boundaries: From Reptilism to Warm-Bloodedness

A serious life means being fully *aware of the alternatives*. It means thinking about them with all intensity one brings to bear on life-and-death questions, in full recognition that every *choice* is a great *risk* with necessarily hard consequences that are hard to bear.

Allan Bloom

The Puzzle Boundaries

When faced with solving a difficult puzzle that contains hundreds of pieces, most people find it helpful to start with the edge pieces. Once these pieces are assembled, it is easier to proceed inward.

This strategy should help us solve the economic and political puzzle in light of the biological parallels. One must realize, however, that the economic puzzle is more complex than the most difficult 2,000-piece puzzle, because the pieces of the economic puzzle keep changing their shapes and colors all the time. To cope with the difficulty, we must fully understand the boundaries. In addition, we must start with the puzzle of the biological systems that are much easier to solve. Then we can translate the solution to our economic and political systems.

Boundaries within Reptilian Systems

We need first to understand the important boundaries within the three basic groups of reptilian systems. In Figure 1, the boundaries are represented as circles. In the real world, however, boundaries may have complex, irregular shapes. The size of each circle represents its "market share" among terrestrial animals. The vertical coordinate of the circle center represents its sophistication level.

In Figure 1, the circles of cold-bloodedness and hibernation are shown as a constant size and of the same vertical coordinate for purposes of simplicity. Of course, in reality, they would vary according to the geological times. For instance, during geological periods of tropical climates, the circle of cold-bloodedness expands and shifts up while the circle of hibernation shrinks and moves down. Obviously cold-bloodedness makes more sense than hibernation in hot climates. The opposite is true during Ice Ages as hibernation becomes more appealing.

Between the circles of cold-bloodedness and hibernation, a third circle represents biological systems that mix cold-bloodedness and hibernation. Note that the circle of mixed systems has a higher center than each of the circles of cold-bloodedness and hibernation. The reason is that there is more intelligence and sophistication in the moderate middle that tries to mix, match and compromise than the extreme left and the extreme right of the biological spectrum.

Let's practice and apply what we've learned to boundaries between economic and political systems. We'll see how this can help solve the most challenging puzzle in the world.

We need first to understand boundaries within reptilian economic and political systems. We still can use Figure 1 to demonstrate these boundaries after adjusting the labels from biological systems to economic systems. Let us concentrate in this chapter on the American version of hibernation as practiced by

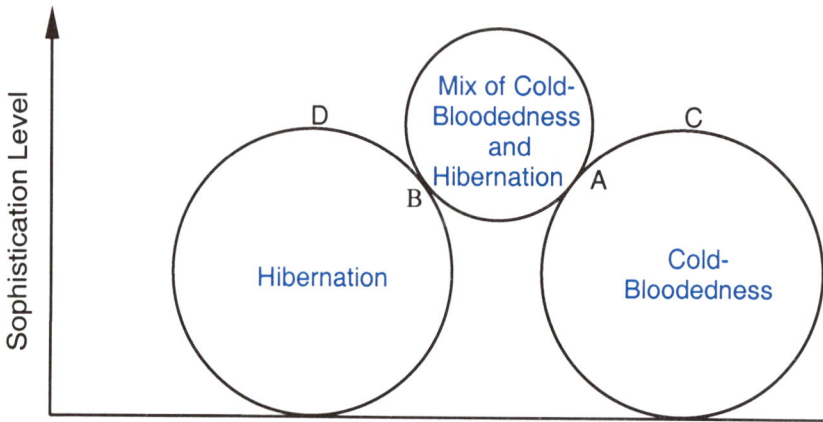

Figure 1: Boundaries Within Reptilian Systems.

Note: For Economic and political applications, replace "Cold-bloodedness" with "Conservatism", "Hibernation" with "Liberalism", and "Mix of Cold-Bloodedness and Hibernation" with "Independent Movement."

liberal Democrats rather than the deeper levels of socialist or communist hibernation. The size of each circle represents its appeal and market share among voters.

In Figure 1, the circles of conservatism and liberalism are of constant size and of the same vertical coordinate for the sake of simplicity. A cold-blooded animal would of course draw Figure 1 differently, raising and enlarging the circle of conservatism, and lowering and shrinking the circle of liberalism. A hibernating animal would redraw Figure 1 in exactly the opposite way. Obviously animals have a hidden instinct to recognize their closest human relatives and be biased to the species that have much in common with them!

Regardless of what animals and humans would think about the circles of conservatism and liberalism, their size would vary according to economic climates. For instance, during periods of relatively warm economic conditions, the circle of conservatism expands and shifts up while the circle of liberalism shrinks and moves down. The opposite is true during Ice Ages such as the Great Depression, when liberalism becomes more appealing.

Between the circles of conservatism and liberalism, the third circle represents a mix of conservatism and liberalism, or what we call the *moderate middle*. This includes the *moderates, liberal conservatives, conservative liberals, swing voters, Independents* and *Reformists*. Note that the circle of these mixed groups has a higher center than each of the circles of conservatism and liberalism. The reason is that there is more intelligence and sophistication in the moderate middle that tries to mix, match, and compromise than the extreme left and extreme right of the economic and political spectrum, although such intelligence is not appreciated yet by most people.

In Figure 1, the circles of conservatism and liberalism do not touch. This means conservatives and liberals hate each other and try to avoid any kind of contact. On the other hand, the circles of conservatism and liberalism both come into contact with the circle of the Independent/Reformist movement at point A and point B respectively. These contact points have relatively high intelligence levels, but not the highest. The circle of conservatism has a point, C, that corresponds to higher intelligence than point A. However, the conservatives of point C abuse their intelligence. They try to deceive their audience with clever arguments exaggerating the advantages of economic cold-bloodedness and bashing any kind of mix or compromise.

The opposite is true for liberals of point D. They give equally clever arguments exaggerating the advantages of economic hibernation and bashing any mix or compromise. But in neither case do these deceptive sermons yield any practical, useful results. For that, one must go to the moderate middle, where intelligence and sophistication are used more wisely to mix and match cold-blooded conservatism and hibernating liberalism.

What is Warm-Bloodedness?

Warm-bloodedness is a biological system in which animals maintain a constant body temperature and high activity rate regardless of the external environment. A warm-blooded animal retains the ability to use the free behavioral options of a cold-blooded reptile—like moving into or away from the sun—to help maintain a comfortable body temperature, but does not depend solely on these options. The warm-blooded animal is equipped with an advanced biological thermostat in its brain called hypothalamus. This thermostat applies automatic feedback control and does not interfere with free behavior or with consciousness.

Defining warm-bloodedness in economic and political terms is much more challenging. *At present, there is no single warm-blooded economic and political system in the entire world.* All systems are reptilian. One needs vision, imagination and ideas drawn by analogy from biological systems to define economic and political warm-bloodedness.

I'll volunteer a definition. I have to admit, however, that *my definition of economic warm-bloodedness is just one definition, not the only one.* Others may come up with different definitions. We need to be open-minded about it. No theory, however, can be a substitute for the actual experience. As we design and build the first generation of warm-blooded economic and political systems, we will learn more from these experiments and get smarter. Then, we can reach a more inclusive and solid definition of economic warm-bloodedness.

In my own interpretation, *warm-bloodedness is an economic system in which the economy maintains constant inflation rates, interest rates, currency rates, unemployment rates and economic activity regardless of the external environment!* Business cycles, recessions and periods of inflation fevers will be things of the dark reptilian past. Not only will we achieve steadiness and stability in economic figures, but we will break new records nobody has even dreamt of, up to now. Those who doubt this possibility are reminded that warm-blooded mammals and birds were able to break new record levels of activity and energy many times higher than reptiles!

In a warm-blooded economic system, the inflation rate will be around two percent, unemployment rate around three percent, and economic growth will reach double figures. A warm-blooded economy will retain all free options afforded by private enterprise. It will also be classified as a free economy, like cold-blooded capitalism. However, the difference between a warm-blooded economy and a capitalist economy will be similar to the difference between a mammal (or a bird) and a cold-blooded reptile!

To apply warm-bloodedness in economics and politics, one must realize that freedom of individuals and firms is at odds with the discretionary power of elected officials and government bureaucrats, including the President, economic advisors of the President, members of Congress, and the chairman and governors of the Federal Reserve Board. In a warm-blooded economy all these bureaucrats will have to give up their decision-making power in operating the economy! Their role in economic policy will be replaced by economic thermostats or what biologists may call economic hypothalamus!

The economic thermostats will be *computer software implementing automatic feedback control concept to regulate economic activity.* They will be similar to *hypothalamus* that regulate body energy in warm-blooded animals, and heating and air-conditioning thermostats regulating home temperatures. Economic thermostats will be designed and marketed by competing firms in the private sector looking mainly for profits. The firms may sell their economic thermostats to both the government and to interested voters who might like to experiment with them or verify their claims in a simulation mode. Individuals may buy the economic thermostat software for something like $30, while the government will have to pay several million dollars per year to apply it to economic policy.

The developers of economic thermostats will not be able to deceive their customers like politicians do, since such practices do not work in free enterprise in the long run. Instead, they will need to look for smart ways to enhance their products and impress their customers. Ross Perot explained the difference between the style of free enterprise and that of government bureaucracy in his book *United We Stand: How We Can Take Back Our Country*:

> In business, people are held accountable. In Washington, nobody is held accountable. In business, people are judged on results. In Washington, people are measured by their ability to get reelected.

During election times, voters will have the freedom to choose the thermostat they prefer, based on past results and the reputation of the firm that produces it. The ability of politicians to deceive voters will no longer be a factor. Voters will be able to choose from American thermostats or from thermostats designed by foreign firms. By the same token, American thermostats will compete in open foreign markets. This means that superior economic thermostats will be within the reach of people anywhere in the world.

Revisions to the thermostats will be allowed only on election days. Beta versions may be tested and reviewed by individuals and consumer magazines before production versions are released. The Beta versions cannot be used, however, in actual economic policy. The main job of government bureaucrats would be to make sure that the thermostat's decisions are implemented properly, whether they personally agree with them or not.

Developing and revising economic thermostats and marketing related products will grow to an industry with a big market. A new branch of macroeconomics will be born to provide academic support for this industry. It will be called *Bio-Economic Engineering* and will blend information and ideas from economics, biology and engineering in revolutionary and creative ways. Professionals who master the new discipline will be called *bio-economic engineers*. They will compete against typical economists the same way mammals and birds competed against dinosaurs before their great extinction. Careers in the field of bio-economic engineering will attract the best brains in the world, and warm-blooded economic and political dreams, that are impossible according to our present reptilian standards, will be realized!

Boundaries between Mixed Reptilism and Warm-Bloodedness

Mixed reptilian systems and warm-blooded systems have things in common. They evolved to fill critical needs. While cold-blooded systems score well in freedom of choice and enjoyment of life, they flunk as far as preserving life in cold climates is concerned. With hibernation systems, it's the other way around. But achieving a good score in one area and flunking in another one is not good enough, no matter how impressive the first score.

Therefore, mixed systems and warm-blooded systems were needed to achieve passing scores in all important areas.

It was the mixed systems that appeared first. They achieved reasonable success within the reptile class, but only up to a certain point. The animal kingdom needed more. Instead of relying on a primitive mix and match of cold-bloodedness and hibernation, the warm-blooded systems developed something more advanced and more sophisticated: the automatic feedback control of blood temperature and energy levels. With such revolutionary change, these animals separated themselves from the reptile class and created a new identity in the form of bird and mammal classes.

The evolution of warm-blooded economic and political systems will be similar to the evolution of warm-blooded biological systems. At present, the only available choice is a mix of cold-blooded conservatism and hibernating liberalism. This choice tries to solve the economic and political dilemma using the democratic process to mix and match. As we have seen, the mix and match has two types: intensity and seasonal, and is mainly influenced by groups of the middle we call moderates, liberal conservatives, conservative liberals, swing voters, Independents and Reformists.

The size of the moderate groups is large enough to determine who wins and who loses in every election. But in spite of their size and influence, moderates do not have a clear political identity or a good size party to represent them. They are abused by our reptilian economic and political system. Regardless of such abuse, the moderates sincerely try their best to steer politics and economics in the right direction. When they think the economic climate is warm and there is a need for cold-blooded conservatism, many of them vote Republican. When they think the climate is cold and there is a need for hibernating liberalism, they tend to vote Democratic. When they are confused, they vote for both.

Mix and match, as practiced by the moderates, has achieved reasonable success, but only up to a certain point. We humans need warm-bloodedness in our economic and political systems; an automatic feedback control of economic metabolism using a design philosophy similar to biological thermostats.

With such revolutionary change, the new class of the warm-blooded middle will have to separate itself from voting within the reptile class that includes the Republican and Democratic Parties. The new warm-blooded class will create a new version of the current Reform Party called the *Warm-Blooded Reform Party*. This will trigger a worldwide *Warm-Blooded Revolution* as all civilized nations create their own versions of warm-blooded parties.

How will those superior warm-blooded species evolve from reptilian species? In Figure 2, cross point E shows where warm-blooded economic and political systems and mixed reptilian systems will separate. As shown in the figure, the supporters of economic warm-bloodedness will first evolve from the moderate middle rather than from typical conservatives and liberals.

Although the oval of economic and political warm-bloodedness in Figure 2 features a new, different profile with broad base and vision, it will start relatively humbly. Time, however, will be on its side. The warm-blooded oval will continue growing in size and sophistication. Such expansion will not come out of nowhere. It will be at the expense of shrinking the three other reptilian circles.

Boundaries between Cold-Bloodedness and Warm-Bloodedness

As the oval of biological warm-bloodedness continued to expand, it came in contact with the circles of cold-bloodedness and hibernation at points F and G respectively, as shown in Figure 2. Such points of contact represent the common boundaries between warm-bloodedness on one side and cold-bloodedness and hibernation on the other side.

At the common boundary of contact point F, warm-bloodedness came to challenge cold-bloodedness face to face in the areas of freedom of choice and enjoyment of living. Up to that point, cold-bloodedness had scored the highest in these areas. But warm-bloodedness demonstrated that automatic feedback control systems do not interfere with freedom and enjoyment of life. On the contrary, the new warm-blooded thermostats helped mammals and birds achieve the highest scores in these areas ever recorded in the history of life.

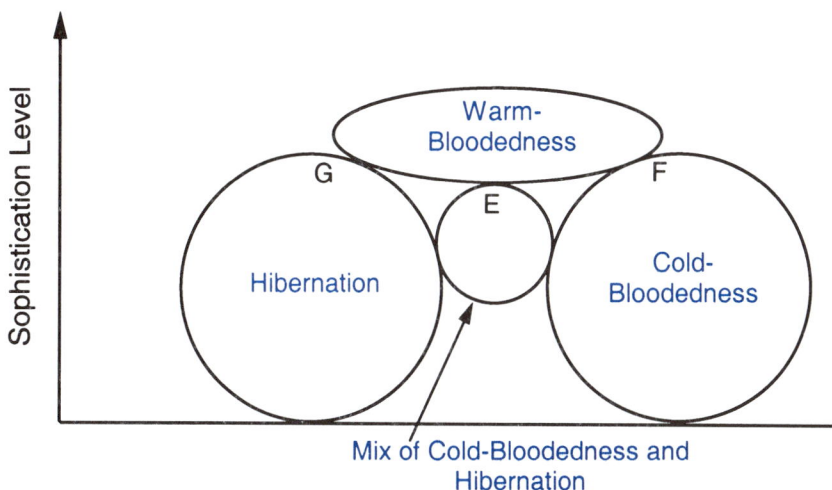

Figure 2: Boundaries Between Reptilian and Warm-Blooded Systems.

Note: For Economic and political applications, replace labels according to Note of Figure 1. Also, make sure to replace "Warm-Bloodedness" with "Future Warm-Blooded Economic/Political Movement."

Economic and political developments will have similar characteristics. As the oval of the new warm-blooded movement continues to expand, it will challenge conservatism in the areas of freedom of choice and empowering people and private enterprise. At present, cold-blooded conservatism's high score in these areas is its only winning ticket. Conservatives, therefore, emphasize freedom more than anything else and consider themselves its only legitimate defenders.

The warm-blooded movement will share many of the conservative values regarding freedom. Conservatives believe that the discretionary power of policymakers undermines economic and political freedom. Warm-blooded proponents will add that such discretion cannot reach the discretion level of a cold-blooded reptile in regulating its blood temperature, for at least four main reasons.

First, reptiles are sincere when they make discretionary decisions to expose their body to the sun or to retreat into the shade. Therefore, they have reasonable success in stabilizing their blood temperature. But politicians, on the contrary, are dishonest, opportunistic and more cold-blooded even than reptiles. They are prone to pursuing their self-interest rather than the well-being of the public and the economy. Even the few honest politicians find it hard to swim against the strong current of special interest groups and the erratic waves of the political process.

Second, reptiles have competent knowledge of the options that would raise or lower blood temperature. On the other hand, policymakers are incompetent. The majority of politicians do not have sufficient economic knowledge to make informed decisions. President John F. Kennedy once admitted that the only way he could remember that the Federal Reserve Board controlled monetary policy, not fiscal policy, was that Chairman McChesny Martin's name began with the letter "M."[1] Presidents are not alone in their limited knowledge. Even governors and chairmen of the Federal Reserve are likely to flunk a simple biological quiz about cold-bloodedness, hibernation, warm-bloodedness, biological thermostats and their equivalents in the habitats of economics and politics. They may not have the slightest idea about the effectiveness of automatic feedback control concept in biology or that there is a need for something similar in macroeconomics policy instead of the current discretionary practice.

Third, in spite of their sluggishness, reptiles act reasonably fast to raise or lower their blood temperature. Policymakers do not. Government decision-making is slow, complex and bureaucratic. It takes many months from the beginning of a recession or inflation to when policymakers become aware of it. There is another lag between the time the need for action is recognized and the time it is actually taken. The combination of both lags can typically amount to well over a year and may occasionally reach two years.

Fourth, reptiles do one effective thing at a time to raise or lower their blood temperature. Policymakers do several things that may contradict each other! For instance, the Federal Reserve may try to slow down the economy by increasing interest rates while the Congress speeds it up by cutting taxes for political reasons! The latter situation cannot be explained by comparison to reptiles. It's like having a car with two irresponsible drivers, one pressing on the gas and the other on the brake at the same time! Such insane practice is lousy for gas mileage, performance, handling and safety. Lack of consistency between the Executive Branch, the Congress and the Federal Reserve is like operating a car with multiple irresponsible drivers. When a fatal accident happens (every recession is a fatal accident), it is impossible to objectively find out who is responsible. As Ross Perot said, "Modern politics has become little more than shirking responsibility and blaming somebody else."

For all these four reasons, cold-blooded reptiles would feel insulted if their discretion in controlling blood temperature is compared to government discretion in controlling the economy! The latter is much more disappointing! Conservative economists, therefore, believe that the discretion of politicians and the Federal Reserve Board cannot be trusted to formulate and carry out successful economic policy. Warm-blooded proponents will strongly agree with conservatives on such issues.

The failure of government discretionary policy lead some conservative economists to advocate taking away discretionary power from politicians and the Federal Reserve Board and replacing it with fixed policy rules. The famous Nobel-prize winner, Milton Friedman, proposed that the optimal monetary policy is to set the growth of the money supply at a fixed rate and hold to that policy throughout all economic conditions. This type of control is a simplistic, *rigid policy rule*. It does not apply the feedback correction principle. A balanced budget amendment is another example of rigid policy rule.

Warm-blooded proponents will agree with conservatives on the failure of *discretionary policy rule* and the need for *automating* government decisions in economic policy to achieve *speed, simplicity and confidence,*[2] instead of current government discretion that is *slow, complex* and *unworthy of trust*. Warm-blooded proponents, however, will disagree on replacing government discretion with only simplistic, rigid policy rules. Warm-blooded thermostats in mammals and birds apply automatic feedback control. Only hibernating animals use rigid control. Therefore, automatic feedback policy rule must also be given a fair chance to compete against conservative rigid policy rules. Fair competition between sophisticated feedback control and simplistic rigid control is provided for animals in the jungle. We humans deserve similar fair competition in our economic and political systems.

The coming warm-blooded movement should not be too preoccupied with finding the right solution or even promoting the idea of automatic feedback control. Instead, the movement should concentrate first on creating the right political environment in which as many solutions as possible—both reptilian and warm-blooded—compete on equal ground. Then, the right solution will eventually prove itself. The warm-blooded movement should trust voters' judgment in electing economic policy directly instead of allowing unlimited government discretion. Voters' judgment may not be perfect, but it is definitely much better than government discretion. And voters will get smarter as they experiment with new economic thermostats.

To simplify things for citizens when they cast their votes on how to run the economy, any proposed economic policy to stabilize business cycles should be called an *economic thermostat*. The thermostats will come in many packages under different brand names.

Some thermostats will use *automatic feedback control logic* similar to the thermostats of warm-blooded animals and those of heating and air-conditioning units. Feedback control logic means that government discretion must be entirely eliminated and replaced by automatic actions triggered by market statistics.

Other thermostats will use *rigid control logic*—like Milton Friedman's thermostat or a balanced-budget thermostat—which means government discretion is replaced by simplistic rigid rules that decide how actions are turned on or off. Unlike feedback control, these rules are not related to varying market statistics.

Voters may also select the option of *"no thermostat,"* which will let *government discretionary control* and the Federal Reserve Board make decisions for economic policy, just as we have at present. Beside these three basic choices, some thermostats will mix two or all the three types of control logic: feedback, rigid and government discretion.

In addition to different types of control logic, the thermostat hardware will also vary. Some thermostats will use *monetary* hardware in which economic control is activated by changes in interest rates. Others will use *fiscal* hardware in which economic control is activated by automatic increase or decrease in income taxes. This will not be done for political reasons to impress voters, but to speed up or slow down the economy as needed. In addition, hybrid thermostats will apply a mix of monetary and fiscal control. With variations in control logic and control hardware, the design possibilities of economic thermostats will be numerous.

Current economic policy can be visualized as a *special case* in which all those options are denied and voters are forced into a single choice of *"no thermostat option."* Such practice is unfair, inefficient, and authoritarian. As we allow this, we are continuously slapping the face of freedom and democracy.

But we do not have to allow this anymore, thanks to the Warm-Blooded Reform Party. The party will make constitutional reforms to our government system that will give the people the right to directly elect economic thermostats and let free enterprise play the major role in developing them. This will create more options and more choices to empower the people, remove power from the federal government and terminate its current monopoly in setting economic policy. Such warm-blooded contribution will add a new dimension to the concepts of democracy, freedom, perfect competition and efficiency. No longer will cold-blooded conservatives think of themselves as the only legitimate defenders of these crucial areas! They will have to bow to new warm-blooded champions who will deliver record results in serving conservative values, instead of just talking cynically about how bad and inefficient government system is and doing nothing about it!

Boundaries between Hibernation and Warm-Bloodedness

Just as the circle of biological warm-bloodedness came face to face to challenge the circle of cold-bloodedness at contact point F in Figure 2, it did the same with the circle of hibernation at point G. Warm-bloodedness came to challenge hibernation by demonstrating that automatic feedback control systems can do an excellent job in preserving life in cold climates and even achieve a higher score than reptilian hibernation.

In this way, economic and political warm-bloodedness will challenge hibernating liberalism and defeat it on liberal issues. At present, liberalism achieves the highest score in the area of fairness and in preserving the financial lives of the working class in cold economic climates. Liberals emphasize these issues more than anything else and consider themselves their only legitimate defenders.

The warm-blooded movement will share many liberal ideas concerning the need for more economic fairness and better survival possibilities for the working class. They will disagree, however, on using economic hibernation methods such as big government, more entitlement programs and more piles of complex regulations.

Liberals must recognize that economic hibernation cannot reach the success level of biological hibernation. Hibernating animals can peacefully hibernate as long as nothing would interrupt their long sleep. The situation in economics and politics, however, is different. Cold-blooded conservatives hate hibernating liberalism and will use every opportunity to terminate it regardless of the fatal casualties. Economic hibernation, therefore, is more vulnerable and more disappointing than biological hibernation. Conservatives may seize the presidency any time and replace the liberal hibernation of the executive branch with a mega-dose of cold-bloodedness, even when the economic environment becomes freezing cold!

Sooner or later, the vulnerability of hibernating liberalism to attacks from cold-blooded conservatives will force more liberals to be open to new warm-blooded ways to promote their values of economic fairness. At present, most liberal economists are in favor of government discretion while most conservative economists oppose it. This suggests that most liberal economists will likely be reluctant to accept the idea of an economic thermostat that terminates government discretion in economic policy. Many ordinary liberal citizens, however, may favor the idea. After all, they are more satisfied with their own biological thermostats and their heating and air-conditioning thermostats than with government discretion.

The warm-blooded movement will try to persuade a few open-minded liberal economists to participate in designing economic thermostats that will use the fiscal control that Keynesian economists favor. This will give Keynesian economists their only opportunity to defeat their enemies the cold-blooded monetarists and wipe them completely from existence! They have to understand, however, the concept of automatic feedback control.

In home thermostats, it is the occupants who set the target temperature. Similarly, in economic thermostats of fiscal control, voters will set a target inflation level. If actual inflation is higher than the target level, the economic thermostat will automatically increase income tax in an amount proportional to the difference (something like a change of 1/4 or 1/2 percent in tax rate for every 1 percent difference between target and actual inflation rates). If actual and target inflation are close, the thermostat will change nothing. If actual inflation is lower than target inflation, the thermostat will cut income tax by an amount proportional to the difference. Because of the sensitivity of economic activity to income taxes in what economists call the *multiplier*, small changes in taxes will result in larger changes in demand for goods and services. Such amplified changes should be sufficient to stabilize the economy.

Tax adjustments activated by economic thermostats may be allowed every quarter or any other suitable time interval. The decisions will be computerized and calculated instantaneously once inflation figures are released. All firms will use the newly adjusted rates immediately to calculate income tax withholding of their employees' paychecks. This will ensure that the delay between when inflation figures are calculated and when *every wage earner* sees the difference is no more than a week or two. When individuals submit their income tax forms for the whole year, the average of income tax rates during the four quarters will be used. Discretionary power of the Federal Reserve Board in setting interest rates will be entirely eliminated. Instead, interest levels will be stabilized at the lowest safe level—something comparable to the rates America had in her best economic times during the 1950s, 1960s and some years in the 1990s.

The liberal thermostat will serve economic fairness by assuring that every single taxpayer in the country will have an equal share of the burden of slowing down the economy and an equal reward in speeding it up. This will be in contrast to the present unfair method of changing interest rates. Under this system, burden and reward are unevenly distributed, favoring some groups over others. For instance, increasing interest rates allows creditors to receive more interest income while debtors see less net income after interest payments. Homeowners who chose variable-rate mortgages are pushed toward the edge of foreclosure. Even those who select 15 or 30-year fixed-rate mortgages pay more indirectly. Their interest rates and payments would be significantly lower if the Federal Reserve was prevented from making short-term interest rates swing as wildly as the blood temperature of cold-blooded reptiles!

Individuals are not the only victims of wild swings in interest rates. Corporations suffer as well. Increasing interest rates raises the capital cost of producing goods and services, and such added cost creates secondary inflationary pressure opposite to the intend of the Federal Reserve board! Corporations have to cope with increased capital costs by squeezing the workers more cruelly than would be the case if the economy were to be slowed down by another method. In addition, an increase in interest rates hurts American products competing in foreign markets.

Local and federal governments suffer too from the Federal Reserve system. As interest rates increase, governments have to spend more in interest payments and are under pressure to cut crucial services that lower, middle class and elderly people expect. In addition, changes in interest rates create erratic waves between bond and stock markets, increase their volatility and expose small investors to more risks. Indeed, the swings in stock and bond markets created by the Federal Reserve Board are probably several times more intense than comparable swings in blood temperature of reptiles.

All these unfair practices that lead to the exploitation of debtors, homeowners, students taking college loans, small business, small investors, export industries and the working class can be avoided if the Federal Reserve Board is dismantled, short-term interest rates are stabilized at optimum levels and economic control becomes entirely fiscal by using economic thermostats! The only issue left is whether such fiscally-controlled thermostats are superior to monetary thermostats in terms of speed, simplicity and effectiveness.

With robust designs of fiscally-controlled thermostats, the warm-blooded movement will add a new dimension to economic fairness and the serving of the working class. No longer will hibernating liberals think of themselves as the only legitimate defenders of these crucial areas! They will have to watch out carefully for what the new warm-blooded species can accomplish in serving liberal values, and hopefully learn from them!

Crossing Boundaries

Once the boundaries between reptilism and warm-bloodedness in economics and politics are clarified, informed citizens will wonder whether they should cross them and flee from the reptilian territories of the Republican and Democratic Parties to join the Warm-Blooded Reform Party. They will have to think deeply and weigh the rewards and risks of their decision. Those who dare to cross the boundaries will form three basic migration waves.

The first and largest migration wave will come from the moderate middle crossing the boundaries between mixed reptilism and warm-bloodedness at contact point E as shown in Figure 3. The moderates, Independents and Reformists will be motivated to seek a new economic and political identity. They will be delighted to find out that the new Warm-Blooded Reform Party will be dedicated to serving the warm-blooded middle.

The second migration wave will come from strict conservatives crossing the boundaries between cold-bloodedness and warm-bloodedness at contact point F. Most of these conservatives will not give a damn about liberal values of economic fairness! They will cross the boundaries simply because they will discover that the Warm-Blooded Reform Party can serve conservative values more than any conservative movement in history!

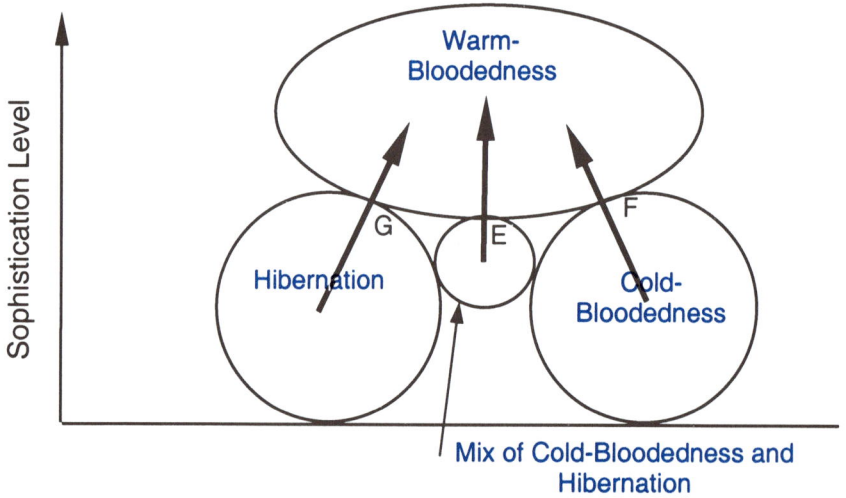

Figure 3: The Three Migration Waves Crossing the Boundaries from
Reptilism to Warm-Bloodedness.

Note: For Economic and political applications, replace labels according
to Notes of Figures 1 and 2.

The third migration wave will come from strict liberals crossing
the boundaries at contact point G. Most of these liberals will not
give a damn about conservative values of economic and political
freedom, either! They will cross the boundaries simply because
they will discover that the Warm-Blooded Reform Party serves their
interests and values better than any liberal movement in history!

With these three migration waves, all individuals with simple
common sense will abandon the current reptilian parties to join
the new Warm-Blooded Reform Party. The reptilian parties will
be left with only those who lack the mental ability to *understand
the boundaries between reptilism and warm-bloodedness in the world of
economics and politics*. This process of *natural selection* will relieve
the Warm-Blooded Reform Party of having to deal with species
that are *too slow to understand,* and pass the responsibility of
taking care of these inferior species to the Republican and
Democratic Parties!

5
Messengers Living Their Messages

There never was an idea started that *woke up men out of their stupid indifference* but its *originator* was spoken of as a *crank*.

Oliver Wendell Holmes, Sr., (1891)

When man has wiped the slate clean and tries to write his own message, the past which lives in him and has molded him will bring back the very things he has tried to obliterate.

Lewis Namier, *Avenue of History*, 1952

Link Between Messages and Messengers

An effective message is more than just an inspiring idea and the right words to express the idea. The messenger is as important as the message, if not more so. For example, if someone is talking about physical fitness, she has to be in good shape to convince the audience. A person who preaches honesty and integrity should have an exemplary record of both in his personal life, otherwise he would sound like a hypocrite. Advice on how to exercise the brain and raise I.Q. would be more effective if developed by people with high I.Q.

Great thinkers who influenced economic and political thoughts throughout history were messengers of new revolutionary ideas. They must have lived their messages in their personal lives to achieve such enormous influence on the history of mankind. The greatest messages delivered so far in modern economics are of the reptilian kind and include: 1) the *message of pure cold-bloodedness*, 2) the *message of deep hibernation*, and 3) the *message of mixing the two*.

To have a better understanding of these three reptilian messages, we need to know more about their messengers and see how they lived their messages in their personal lives. The three giants who delivered these messages had many things in common despite their differences. Each one wrote a masterpiece that made his ideas immortal. These masters tried hard to persuade their contemporaries of the need to evolve into a more advanced form of economic and political thinking. They rejected the conventional wisdom of their day. Because of their revolutionary thinking, they were considered *cranks* by many people and their ideas seemed *ridiculous*. But they did not get discouraged by this unfriendly treatment. Instead, they planted the seeds and waited patiently for their visionary messages to grow in the real world. They died before they could see the full harvest of their hard work, their ideas reaching peak acceptance only after their death.

Message and Messenger of Pure Cold-Bloodedness

The Scottish philosopher and economist Adam Smith (1723-1790) carried the responsibility of delivering the message of pure cold-bloodedness to the world of economic and politics. The message is called *pure capitalism* or *laissez-faire capitalism*. It promotes the idea that the economy should be freed from all forms of government regulations to reach the status of cold-blooded reptiles that are freed from all forms of biological regulations related to blood temperature and body energy!

Smith delivered his message when political and economic systems in Western European nations were moving toward democracy and a market economy. That historical time was similar to the geological time when the few amphibians that had significant reptilian features were evolving to become fully terrestrial reptiles.

To appreciate Smith's economic message, imagine that he had a *biological counterpart* who had lived at the transition period between the end of the Age of Amphibians and the beginning of the Age of Reptiles. Let us call such biological counterpart *Adam Smithosaur*. Adam Smithosaur would have delivered a biological message to introduce the reptilian species. The message would have started with a criticism of all remaining links with amphibianism and then laid the foundation of modern terrestrial living as pioneered by the reptile class.

The real Adam Smith did exactly the same. He opposed all links with mercantilism and government planning of the economy and laid the foundation of modern capitalism.

Smith documented his message in the masterpiece *The Wealth of Nations* in 1776. Many conservatives consider this 900-page masterpiece as the bible of capitalism, and Adam Smith as its prophet or even its God. The full title of Smith's book is *An Inquiry into the Nature and Cause of the Wealth of Nations*. As the title suggests, the book keenly focused on the particular goal of how to achieve and accumulate wealth.

Let's go back to Smithosaur. Now, Smithosaur needs to think of a title of his masterpiece that will introduce the reptilian species to the animal kingdom. He decides on *An Inquiry into the Nature and Cause of the Gigantic Size of the Reptilian Species*. The reason is that one would translate *wealth* to *body size* since wealth is the size of accumulated money.

The titles of both the biological and real books emphasize, respectively, the importance of big wealth in capitalist economies and gigantic body size in cold-blooded reptilian species.

Smith was confident that he had discovered the secrets of accumulating gigantic wealth, and believed his ideas would be relevant forever. Leave the economy free from government intervention, Smith urged, and all economic problems will be solved! He stated that motives of self-interest and individualism were more effective in accumulating wealth than kindness, community concern or altruism.

Smith's personal life was a mirror image of his cold-blooded reptilian message. He was ugly in appearance and cold in feelings. But he had a good side as well. He studied moral philosophy at the Universities of Glasgow and Oxford. After graduation he was appointed professor of logic and later of moral philosophy at Glasgow. His academic achievements could not hide his resemblance to reptiles. Todd G. Buchholz—a conservative economist and former Associate Director of President George Bush's Economic Policy Council—compiled a picture of Smith from various sources:

> Smith was an odd-looking Scotsman. He had a large nose, bulging eyes, a protruding lower lip, a nervous twitch and a speech impediment. Smith once acknowledged his unusual features, saying: "I am a beau in nothing but my books." [1]

Smith never married, in part because of his ugly features and cold feelings. This may not be a good excuse because many unattractive individuals manage to find spouses. Like the extinct dinosaurs, Smith had no descendants. He practiced individualism and selfishness in his personal life too. He never experienced closeness with a woman. His loneliness may had its roots in early childhood as his father died months before his birth.

Shortly before his death, Smith had nearly all his manuscripts destroyed. No one knows for sure what was the intention behind such strange behavior. Maybe it was a mysterious premonition that, like the dinosaurs, his own message, and the economic species of laissez-faire capitalism that he loved the most, was also doomed!

With his weird looks and personality, and cold lifestyle, it would be hard to find another person more qualified than Adam Smith to deliver the message of pure cold-bloodedness in the habitats of economics and politics. This message had a positive impact in accelerating the evolution of modern economies from their amphibian roots to reptilian forms.

Message and Messenger of Deep Hibernation

It was the German economist, philosopher and revolutionist Karl Heinrich Marx (1818-1883) who carried the responsibility of delivering the message of deep hibernation to the habitats of economics and politics. Marx was born 28 years after Adam Smith's death. This illustrates how slow things are in economics. It takes several generations to digest a major message and be ready for the next one.

Marx's message was that the wealth Smith described had accumulated in a few gigantic species, the capitalists, while the majority of the working class had almost nothing. The gigantic species were preying on and exploiting the little ones. The exploited species suffered as many financial deaths in periods of recessions and depressions as those little cold-blooded reptiles faced in ice ages.

To solve these serious problems, Marx urged people to seek deep hibernation in communism. People and nations must give up their economic and political freedom. In return, they will be given better security and more enhanced survival opportunity. But Marx went too far in promoting hibernation solutions. Unlike animals that hibernate out of necessity during the cold season, Marx called for something that exists only in the world of economics and politics: *continuous deep hibernation from cradle to grave, passed from generation to generation!*

Marx delivered his message when capitalism was at an early and clumsy stage. That historical time was similar to the geological time of the first fifty million years of the Age of Reptiles, during which reptilism was at its infancy and had not reached full vigor.

Had there been a Karl Marxosaur during the Age of Reptiles, he would have started by criticizing cold-bloodedness and its failure to preserve little species in ice ages. Marxosaur would emphasize that reptilian species that chose cold-bloodedness would eventually be extinct as the terrestrial environment has no mercy for cold-bloodedness. The biological message would then have described how to install and maintain deep hibernation control systems to increase the likelihood of species' survival.

Marx did exactly the same. He bitterly attacked capitalism and laid the intellectual foundation of communism. Marx documented his hibernation messages in two masterpieces. The first, *The Communist Manifesto*, is a booklet of fewer than forty pages. He wrote it with Friedrich Engels in 1847. Marx was just 29 years old then. If this booklet had had a biological counterpart in the Age of Reptiles, it would have been called *The Manifesto of Continuous Deep Hibernation*. The need for economic and political hibernation was enormous and this was reflected for over a century in the popularity of Marx's book. By 1964, this little booklet had more than 1,000 editions in more than 100 languages with total printings in excess of 14 million copies.

In contrast to the little *Manifesto*, Marx wrote another masterpiece, *Das Kapital*, which was a huge 2,500-page work of four volumes, with citations to more than 1,500 works. If such series had a biological counterpart, it would be called *Das Kold-Blooded Reptiles*.

Marx spent 17 years writing the first volume of *Das Kapital*, which was published in 1867. He did not succeed in producing a finished version of the remaining three volumes although he worked on the manuscripts until his death in 1883. The second and third volumes were edited by Engels and published in 1885 and 1894. The fourth volume was edited by Karl Kautsky and published more than 25 years after Marx's death. *Das Kapital* remains one of the most influential books ever written.

Did Marx's personal life reflect his message of continuous, deep hibernation? The answer is *no* for his early life, but *yes* after graduation from college. Marx had an impressive education and a promising start. He showed intellectual talents in school and went to the universities of Bonn and Berlin where he studied many fields, but focused on philosophy, religion and history. In 1841, Marx obtained his doctorate in philosophy from the University of Jena. In 1843 he married Jenny von Westphalen, daughter of Baron von Westphalen, a highly placed Prussian government official. With superior intelligence, a doctoral degree and a wife from the aristocracy, Marx seemed to have everything needed for an easy, successful life.

Troubles started, however, when Marx joined a group of radical leftist students and professors while still in college. After graduation, he intended to teach philosophy at the university but that quickly proved to be unrealistic. Marx then turned to journalism and became editor of a liberal newspaper. Shortly after his marriage, the government suppressed the paper because of its radical views and strong criticism of the government. Soon, Marx emigrated with his bride to Paris to edit a magazine. The magazine lasted only one issue, perhaps because of Marx' contribution. Despite such disappointment, he found personal satisfaction in making contact with French communists, socialists and working-men's groups. It was there that Marx met his lifelong friend, Friedrich Engels, who collaborated with him on many writings.

After less than two years in Paris, Marx was expelled. He then moved to Brussels, Belgium, where he stayed from 1845 to 1848. As soon as the German Revolution of 1848 broke out, he was in turn expelled from Belgium. He went to Cologne. After the collapse of the revolution, Marx was expelled from Prussia and never succeeded in recovering his citizenship. He migrated to London where he would reside as a political exile until the end of his life.

Marx and his family suffered a lot in the turbulent 1840s, when he was expelled many times. Settling in London did not bring an end to the suffering of a life on the run. It was the beginning of another kind of misery that was slow, long and continuous, with minimum interruptions; something that resembled his hibernation message. Contrary to Marx's hope, he never succeeded in earning enough money from his writing to sustain himself and his growing family of seven children. The only small income he made in London was when he became the European correspondent of the *New York Daily Tribune* in 1851. But this income was not steady, and it ended after ten years.

So the years of Marx's London exile were mainly years of material deprivation and moral suffering. He was hurt by the fact that he could not provide adequate living conditions for his wife and children, whom he loved deeply. His mother once commented, "Karl, I wish you would make some capital instead of just writing about it." Marx never had any affection for his mother, probably because of her nasty comments about his unusual lifestyle.

Todd G. Buchholz (whose description of Smith's ugly appearance was quoted earlier) gives interesting details of Marx's life in London:

> In the 1850s, Marx buried himself in piles of economics texts in the British Museum in London. His family starved while he analyzed the abstract suffering of the proletariat. The Marxs lived in a sleazy apartment in one of the poorest parts of London. A police spy investigating Marx provided an extraordinary vivid portrait of the squalor his family endured:
>
> "When one enters Marx's room, the eyes get so dimmed by coal smoke and tobacco fumes that for the first moments one gropes as if in a cave...Everything is dirty, everything full of dust, sitting down becomes a truly dangerous business. Here stands a chair with only three legs, there the children play and prepare food on another chair which happens to be still whole."
>
> As for Marx himself, "he is a highly disorderly, cynical person, a poor host; he leads a real gypsy existence. Washing, grooming and changing underwear are rarities with him; he gets drunk readily. Often he loafs all day long, but if he has work to do, he works day and night tirelessly." [2]

In five wretched years in London, Marx lost three children to pneumonia, bronchitis and tuberculosis. Perhaps what happened to Marx's children was an indirect message of what may happen to nations that give up everything for economic and political hibernation. Hibernation may not save their people.

Marx suffered from frequent illnesses, many of which may have been psychological as a result of the loss of his children and extreme poverty. Even when physically healthy, he suffered from long periods of apathy and depression. This should be expected from a sophisticated person with a doctorate who could not earn sufficient money to support his family and had to get financial help from his lifelong friend Friedrich Engels—who happened to be the son of a wealthy textile manufacturer .

Marx's personal life reflects the typical history of communism. Communism starts with turbulent periods in a nation's history similar to the period of hardship during the 1840s, in which Marx had to flee from one European city to the other. Such turbulence creates a sense of insecurity, anger and desperation. This stage prepares the nation to give up freedom and accept the false hope of security through communism. When the nation settles finally for the hibernation coma of communism, its political and economic life becomes as dull and depressing as Marx's life in London.

If there had been a contest with a million dollar prize to find the person whose personal life most resembles deep hibernation, the winner would probably have been Marx. With his rare personal qualifications, Marx was fit to deliver the message of deep hibernation. Such a message provided the opportunity for humans to experiment with deep hibernation and see if it satisfied their economic and political needs. The human participants were many. By 1960, the nations of one third of the world population claimed to have adopted Marxist hibernating ideas.

Message and Messenger of Mixing Pure Cold-Bloodedness and Deep Hibernation

The British liberal economist John Maynard Keynes (1883-1946) delivered the message of mixing pure cold-bloodedness and deep hibernation to the habitats of economics and politics. Such contribution qualified him as the most influential economist of the twentieth century. Keynes was born the same year Marx died. This was quite an improvement: the new messenger arrived faster when compared with his predecessor Karl Marx who was born 28 years after Adam Smith's death.

Keynes's message is known as Keynesian economics. The message is that there are times when pure capitalism would be as vulnerable as the biological systems of cold-blooded reptiles caught in an ice age. In order to preserve the financial lives of millions of people who wanted to work but could not find jobs, Keynes suggested a new, smaller dose of liberal hibernation, described as government discretionary intervention in the economy through tax and spending policy. Keynes claimed that a small hibernation dose would be sufficient to save financial lives of workers. He was looking for a reasonable mix and compromise between pure laissez-faire cold-bloodedness and deep communist hibernation.

Keynes delivered his message at the height of the Great Depression. His luck was unbelievable. There could not have been a better time to deliver it. From 1929 to 1933, unemployment in the U.S. exploded from three percent to 25 percent, and national income plunged by half. Many lost their homes and businesses. Workers scrambled for the few jobs available. As psychological depression accompanied economic depression, more individuals, politicians and economists were receptive to Keynes' moderate hibernation recipe.

In order to understand and appreciate Keynes' message, we need to simplify it with a biological analogy. Let us travel back in time to the middle of the Age of Reptiles, even though the Age of Reptiles is too good to represent the world of modern economics and politics. During the Age of Reptiles there were mammal-like reptiles, bird-like reptiles, and even mammals and birds. There was as yet nothing as advanced as those species in the world of economics and politics during Keynes' time. We need to adjust for this difference. Let us assume that the imaginary Age of Reptiles has been mysteriously altered to include only reptilian species as primitive and inferior as those in economics and politics. The choices would be either pure cold-bloodedness the Adam Smithosaur's way or deep hibernation the Karl Marxosaur's way. Then, an ice age as severe and as long as the Great Depression arrives to put those species to the ultimate test.

All reptiles equipped with pure cold-blooded systems experience a large drop in their blood temperature and many of them died. The few surviving species are scared to death. They are likely to feel cheated that the cold-blooded reptilian systems did not perform as well as what Adam Smithosaur claimed. But reptiles equipped with deep hibernation systems have the opposite experience. If they are awakened to look at the horrible catastrophe, they would cheer up. At last, the prophecy of Karl Marxosaur, that the cold-blooded reptilian systems would end in great mass extinction, is happening.

Now let us imagine a counterpart of Keynes is sent to the animals to help them in their struggle for survival. We may call such a counterpart Keynesosaur. Keynesosaur has mixed feelings. There is compelling evidence that pure cold-blooded designs are vulnerable in ice ages. Still, Keynesosaur thinks that settling for the coma of continuous, deep hibernation is too much as the animals are deprived of a conscious sense of living. Finally, he arrives at a logical compromise between both extremes, although his solution is closer to pure cold-bloodedness than deep hibernation. That solution is called Keynesosaur's moderate hibernation of the drowsy kind, and it is supposed to save reptilian species from mass extinction.

Although Keynesosaur's teachings make sense from a practical point of view, he faces two philosophical arguments from followers of pure cold-bloodedness, who regard him as a dangerously radical crank. First, the cold-blooded conservatives are reluctant to accept even the smallest dose of hibernation to save life. Keynesosaur yells at the skeptics who cannot compromise:

> I defend moderate hibernation... both as the only practical means of avoiding the great mass extinction catastrophe of existing reptilian species and as the condition of their successful future survival. [3]

The second argument is aimed at Keynesosaur's proposal that lets a deficit in energy spending accumulate during hibernation. Proponents of pure cold-bloodedness cherish a balanced energy budget amendment. This balance means the total energy spent by a cold-blooded reptile during any season must not exceed the energy of food intake. Reptiles can adhere easily to this policy during tropical climates of lush vegetation and plenty of prey. There are problems, however, during ice ages when food sources are scarce and hard to find. At the same time, energy spending is too high because of increased heat loss to surroundings. The conventional cold-blooded reptilian wisdom still insists on a balanced energy budget no matter how little the food sources are and how cold the environment gets. To achieve such balance, metabolism must be reduced. The reduction in metabolism would lower the blood temperature, body energy and the ability of animals·to move. A slow and weak animal finds less food. But still a balanced energy policy calls for cutting metabolism even more. Such a spiral would get worse and worse until the animal finally dies.

The tragic scene of the mountains of dead animals breaks the heart. With tears pouring heavily from his eyes, Keynesosaur looks sadly at their bodies wondering what good freedom and the strict application of a balanced energy budget are when the result is loss of life. He reasons that if animals were to hibernate to a moderate level and if this leads to a deficit in energy spending during the hibernation session, so what? Preserving life is much more precious than anything else, even freedom and conscious sense of living. He blasts the views of the cold-blooded conservatives who claim that warm climates are around the corner, and therefore, prescribe patience for a few hundred thousand years or so until the ice age is over and a new tropical age begins!

Still the cold-blooded opponents are not moved either by Keynesosaur's furious argument or by the scene of dead animals. With outrage, he screams at them, *"In the long run, we—the reptilian species—are all dead. "*

Nobody in our imaginary Age of Reptiles would know what Keynesosaur meant by his prophecy. It would only be understood in the light of what happened at the end of the Age of Reptiles when all dinosaurs died and mammals took their place.

After exhausting all arguments, Keynesosaur documents his moderate hibernation message in a book similar to what the real Keynes did. In 1936, the real Keynes published his masterpiece *The General Theory of Employment, Interest and Money.* Keynesosaur, therefore, should give his biological book the title *The General* Reptilian Theory *of Feeding, Predation and Food.* Such a translation from economic world to biological world is expected. Employment and jobs feed economies and individuals alike. Interest determines how the predatory and scavenging species in the society prey and feed on the working class. Money is simply food; without it people would starve financially.

Having covered the story of Keynesosaur, let's go back to the real Keynes' book. Unlike Adam Smith's 900-page *Wealth of Nations* and Karl Marx's 2500-page *Das Kapital*, Keynes' book *The General Theory* was only slightly larger than average. Keynes loaded the book with complex equations sprinkled with Greek symbols like those found in books of advanced mathematics. He wrote for professional economists rather than a lay audience. Paul Samuelson, a loyal disciple of Keynes and a Nobel-prize winner whose introductory economics text has taught Keynesian economics to generations, cleverly summed up the paradox of the *General Theory*:

> It is a badly written book, poorly organized; any layman who, beguiled by the author's previous reputation, bought the book was cheated of his five shillings.... It is arrogant, bad tempered, polemical and not overly generous in its acknowledgments. It abounds in mares' nests and confusions.... In short, it is a work of genius. [4]

Keynes' style of mixing is demonstrated in his book, with its mixture of bad writing, ambiguity and brilliance. The long title of the book does not convey a clear message like *The Wealth of Nations* or *Das Kapital*, but a vague mix of several things. Keynes' career was an unusual mix of many things. In addition to his work as an influential economist, he was—often simultaneously—a high government official, an editor of an academic journal, a businessman managing his investment, a professor at Cambridge University, a college bursar, a collector of rare books, a patron of the arts, a member of the House of Lords, and a leading member of English intellectual and cultural circles.

Of all the numerous mixes in Keynes' life, none was as dramatic as his mix of homosexuality and marrying a woman. Paul Krugman, a Keynesian economist, reported that *"Conservatives dislike Keynes because he was aesthete and homosexual."* [5] William Greider confirmed this in his bestseller, *Secrets of the Temple:*

> Despite his Cambridge education, aristocratic manner and wealth, Keynes was also an outsider in his own

way. He was an aesthete who enjoyed describing himself as an "immoralist," a leading member of the sparkling circle of British intellectuals known as the Bloomsbury group that defied Victorian mores in both art and love. Keynes was married but also homosexual, a fact that automatically puts him in defiance of social convention. [6]

When Keynes married Lydia Lopokova, a Russian ballerina, he was 42 years old. They had no children from their marriage. Keynes must have been smart; he would not have proposed to a British woman who would know the rumors about his homosexual adventures. Keynes' lifestyle, mixing and reconciling homosexuality and conventional marriage, is a mirror of the economic and political views of his liberal followers who mix and reconcile pure cold-bloodedness of the laissez-faire kind and deep hibernation of the communist kind. What conservatives and communists feel about liberals and their affairs with both of them at the same time must be similar to what a cheated wife and homosexual lover felt about Keynes who described himself as an immoralist.

But he was certainly the person best qualified to mix and reconcile things that most people would never dare to think about in the same breath. So it was he who delivered the message of mixing and reconciling pure cold-bloodedness and deep hibernation to the world of economics and politics.

From the 1936 publication of the *General Theory* to the Nixon years, Keynes' views of moderate hibernation became widely accepted among economists in England, the U.S. and numerous other countries, while his conservative critics were in the minority. Keynesian influence reached its peak when Nixon—who as a Republican President was supposed to follow cold-blooded conservatism—announced, *"We are all Keynesian now."* Nixon probably had no idea about Keynes's personal lifestyle, especially in things related to homosexuality!

Ironically, not long after Nixon's statement, Keynesian ideas were challenged by conservatism and gradually lost their influence. The generation that saw the horrors of the Great Depression was replaced by another that perceived no need for any kind of

Keynesian hibernation and had no idea about the risks associated with cold-blooded conservatism.

Message and Messenger of Warm-Bloodedness

The fourth message, which has yet to be delivered to the world of modern economics and politics, is the message of warm-bloodedness. The message is that all current economic and political systems in the world resemble reptiles. Some systems lean more toward pure cold-bloodedness, some toward deep hibernation, and others toward a mix of cold-bloodedness and hibernation. None of these reptilian systems will ever satisfy us as warm-blooded humans. The only satisfaction will come from seeking and achieving warm-bloodedness in economics and politics. Warm-bloodedness means more economic and political freedom, eliminating business cycles and running the economy at a steady level of vigor similar to that of warm-blooded mammals and birds as compared to motionless reptiles.

The rationale of this message is that because warm-blooded biological systems are superior to reptilian ones, warm-blooded economic and political systems must also be superior. So far, instead of learning from animal experience and applying their lessons to our economic and political systems, we have relied on philosophical arguments that have little to do with reality. During the last two centuries, we have conducted dangerous economic and political experiments on ourselves. We came up with ridiculous, reptilian systems that are much more inferior to the biological systems of animals during the Age of Reptiles!

Let us then try to be humble and admit our failures and limitations. Let us understand the biological solutions God and nature offered to us. Let us investigate whether or not these biological solutions are applicable to our economic and political systems. After all, such solutions have been tried and continuously tested for many millions of years to reach perfection.

Economists, in general, cannot translate solutions from biological systems to economic and political systems because of their limited understanding of science and technology. Therefore, they need biologists and engineers who have scientific and technological expertise. Most biologists and engineers, however, have too little knowledge about economics. There is a need, therefore, for adventurous economists, biologists and engineers to team up, share their knowledge and evolve into a new breed of professionals called *bio-economic engineers*. These professionals will lay the foundation of a new discipline called *bio-economic engineering*.

The birth of bio-economic engineering will be a major breakthrough, a new beginning in the successful crossbreeding of social and natural sciences. Other disciplines resulting from such crossbreeding will follow soon.

The new discipline of bio-economic engineering will radiate the message of warm-bloodedness in academia. Such a message, however, cannot afford to be limited only to scholars and to isolate itself behind academic walls. The message has to reach out to ordinary people and explain complex economic and political issues in simple language that voters understand. Typically, political parties take care of explaining economic issues, but after some distortion. The parties act like sales agents or distributors of economic schools of thoughts to ordinary citizens.

The Republican Party markets pure cold-blooded conservatism. The Democratic Party sells hibernating liberalism. With both existing parties committed to reptilian schools of thought, there is a need to establish a new version of the Reform Party committed only to economic and political warm-bloodedness. This first version will be called *The Warm-Blooded Reform Party*. Following the American lead, many warm-blooded parties will spring up in other countries around the world. Those parties will endorse the right of people to directly elect economic thermostats to eliminate the current monopoly of federal governments and central banks in setting economic policies, which result in much abuse.

The new warm-blooded parties will coordinate their effort in a multi-national organization called *The International Coalition of Warm-Blooded Parties* with its headquarters in Washington and satellite branches in many capitals around the world. This organization will let parties share intelligence and experience, and give moral support to newly established parties. It will also organize the attack on existing reptilian parties to achieve the final goal of freeing all humans around the world from the burden of economic and political reptilism.

The reptilian parties, both conservative and liberal, will have to defend themselves against the new threat from rising warm-blooded parties. Reptilian humans cannot sit back doing nothing as they watch themselves go extinct. Conservative parties led by the Republican Party will establish a new organization called *The International Coalition of Cold-Blooded Reptilian Parties*. Liberal parties, too, led by the Democratic Party will establish *The International Coalition of Hibernating Parties*.

But this will not be sufficient to defend reptilian economic and political systems. The coalitions will have to go a step further and consolidate their troops under a single commanding organization called *The International Consolidation of Reptilian Parties*.

With these developments, by the early years of the new millennium, *World War III* will start. A brutal fight between warm-bloodedness and reptilism will take place in every nation. Unlike earlier world wars, in which tens of millions of people were killed, the new world war will feature not a single bullet fired or single drop of blood shed. The battles will be entirely intellectual. Instead of weapons of destruction, the new war will be fought with weapons of construction—namely human creative thoughts.

The most critical battle will be fought in Washington. During the election year 2000, the first warm-blooded candidates for presidency and Congress will arise. For the first time in human history, the voters will have the opportunity to elect warm-blooded species in the habitats of economics and politics.

One should not dwell on an immediate victory for the new Warm-Blooded Reform Party. Things may take time. Warm-blooded animals didn't conquer dinosaurs immediately; it took them more than a hundred million years from their first appearance to the time they defeated reptiles at the end of the Cretaceous Period. We should expect the warm-blooded economic and political species to take a long time, too, before they win. Obviously it won't be as long as 100 million years. We humans must do better than animals. My own prediction is that the Warm-Blooded Reform Party will achieve its first victory no later than the year 2008. Regardless of whether the victory takes place in 2000, 2004 or 2008, our descendants will always remember the year when the first Warm-Blooded President and Warm-Blooded Congress replace the reptilian ones and dismantle the Federal Reserve Board.

Following the victory of warm-bloodedness and defeat of reptilism, the American people will trust nothing but warm-blooded species in economics and politics. The reptilian parties, Republican and Democratic, will go extinct. So will the Federal Reserve Board.

The triumph of warm-bloodedness and defeat of reptilism in Washington will trigger similar events in many capitals around the world. This will mark the beginning of the *Worldwide Warm-Blooded Revolution*. Finally, the current *Dark Age of Reptilian Economics and Politics* will have to yield to a new, *Bright Age of Mammalian Economics and Politics*.

The message of warm-bloodedness is a combination hope and dream; it is a daring idea of copying warm-blooded solutions provided by God and nature in biology in the realm of economics and politics; an attempt to crossbreed natural and social sciences into new exciting disciplines; and a prophecy based on logical and scientific reasoning.

The warm-blooded message has been already delivered at the beginning of the new millennium. The arrival of the new millennium is only a couple of months after the *seventieth anniversary of the Great Depression*.

Such critical time is similar to the last few million years of the Age of Reptiles. Reptiles had no idea what the future was hiding for them. At that time, reptilism reached full vigor and things seemed perfect for reptiles. There were no messages to warn them against the great catastrophe that would wipe out all the dinosaurs and many other reptilian species. And even if they could have understood warnings, there wouldn't have been enough time for them to evolve into warm-blooded species.

Humans at the beginning of the new millennium face a dilemma similar to that the reptiles encountered at the end of their age. The current economic environment seems perfect and there haven't been better economic times for a long time. We, however, should be smart enough to understand the warnings against current reptilian economics and politics and the need for warm-bloodedness. All the signs are there.

As the third millennium dawns, many people are troubled about economic and political history. We have had the Great Depression of the 1930s. We have had many severe recessions and periods of scary inflation fevers. We have had economic injustice with many innocent victims suffering. Most working, lower and middle class people feel that they are in a slow recession in which their living standards are deteriorating in a pattern too slow to be generally noticeable, despite the impressive economic statistics and the boom of Wall Street. More and more people are fed up with the inability of Republicans and Democrats to solve our serious economic and trade problems. Those people are trapped into negative feelings of helplessness and hopelessness despite promising economic statistics. They feel that these statistics must be illusive and deceptive, not reflecting what actually happens to the majority of the working class.

But it is unnatural for humans to start the new millennium with negative feelings. They simply cannot do it. They must have economic and political hope. The warm-blooded message is a *message of hope*. There has never been a better time in the entire human history to deliver such a message. We have tried all possible reptilian solutions in our economic and political systems. Nothing has worked. Nothing will work. We need something drastically different. We need a *quantum leap,* not just a little change here or there. We need a *Worldwide Warm-Blooded Revolution* to bring new hopes to us and our children as the new millennium dawns.

Now humans need warm-bloodedness in economics and politics, and the beginning of the new millennium is a perfect time for the message, who is supposed to deliver it? Before we answer this question we have to recall the previous three reptilian messages and who delivered them. In all three cases, *the messengers lived the messages.* Adam Smith lived the message of economic cold-bloodedness in his ugly features and lonely, cold lifestyle. Karl Marx lived the message of economic hibernation in extreme poverty and material deprivation during his exile in London. John Maynard Keynes lived the message of mixing and reconciling economic cold-bloodedness and hibernation in his unusual lifestyle, which combined homosexuality with marrying a woman. This pattern of the *messengers living their messages* must continue too for the fourth message of warm-bloodedness.

What aspects of warm-bloodedness will its messenger have to live in his personal life? Before answering this question, we need to do a little homework. We need to gather information about early forms of warm-blooded animals. Their lives in such an early period should give us clues about the probable lifestyle of the messenger of warm-bloodedness.

Paleontologists (scientists specializing in studying ancient life forms) believe that mammals were the first warm-blooded vertebrate class. Birds came later. The first true mammals were the *megazostrodon*. The megazostrodons were tiny, inconspicuous, mouse-like creatures which fed on insects after dark. They could not come out by day because they could not compete against the ferocious dinosaurs that could have eaten them.

The messenger of warm-bloodedness in economics and politics should resemble the tiny megazostrodon. He is likely to be small in financial size and assets. Physically, he should be small too. Like nocturnal animals that feed after dark and hide during daytime, he has to work on preparing his message after dark and hide in another job from 8 to 5 to support himself and his family. The hiding hours are often stretched to evenings and weekends to meet the increased pressure for more productivity from workers and more profit margin to deliver to shareholders. As the new millennium approaches, he has to do whatever it takes to deliver the message during such perfect time, no matter how much the pressure he faces in his regular job, even if this means killing himself by working continuously, day and night.

The messenger of warm-bloodedness must know from personal experience how it feels to be a tiny megazostrodon struggling for survival in the Age of Reptiles. The megazostrodons looked hard for food that was mostly insects. Such a diet is little in amount and disgusting in taste. The messenger, too, must precisely feel that. His daily job title, responsibilities and income—compared to what he deserves for preparing and delivering his message—

should resemble the insects the megazostrodons were feeding upon.

As if these things were not bad enough for the messenger, he should also look as inconspicuous as early mice and rats living in the Age of Reptiles. Gigantic dinosaurs would probably look at those tiny mammals as worthless, alien creatures that should be stepped upon or gobbled whole. Dinosaurs had no idea that one day those little mammals would defeat them, force them into mass extinction and inherit the planet!

Likewise, current experts on economics and politics may look at the messenger of warm-bloodedness as an outsider. After all, he has no Ph.D. or even a formal degree in economics to qualify him as an authority, just as the legendary pioneers of aviation and personal computers—the Wright Bothers, Steve Jobs and Bill Gates—did not have a college degree. It wouldn't be easy for the experts to understand the messenger's analogical reasoning approach and his vision of bridging social sciences (economics and politics) with natural sciences and technology (biology and engineering). The experts will be tempted to step on the messenger and gobble him whole. They will have no idea that the professional followers of the messenger, the bio-economic engineers, will one day exterminate typical economists and inherit their habitats!

In living the life of the megazostrodons, the messenger of warm-bloodedness should have an accent as awkward and funny as the Mickey-mouse-type highly-pitched vocalizations of early mammals. Their sounds were like a joke compared to the roaring sounds of the mighty t-rexes and other ferocious carnosaurs that would scare any creature to death.

Despite their hostile surroundings, the megazostrodons were probably playful animals, like their close surviving relatives, the mice and rats. The megazostrodons' lifestyle was likely to be different from the more serious lifestyle of most reptiles. Similarly, the messenger of warm-bloodedness should be more playful in delivering his message. He must be more humorous and entertaining than the three more serious earlier messengers.

The warm-blooded messenger is likely to face as many attacks from current reptilian species as the megazostrodons had faced in defending themselves against the ferocious dinosaurs. The messenger, however, must have *hope* and *faith* in the future. The messenger knows that early mammals did not stay tiny, frightened, inconspicuous and nocturnal forever. Gradually, they increased in body size, became more powerful, gained more confidence, and changed their period of activity from night to day. In like manner, the warm-blooded messenger must see similar developments. The messenger will not stay tiny, frightened, and inconspicuous hiding in a daily job and moon-lighting on his warm-blooded message after dark. He has a dream that one day he will be able to dedicate himself to working full-time on his warm-blooded message, instead of putting it on a second priority after a daily job.

Will these daring prophecies ever happen? Will the message of economic and political warm-bloodedness ever reach out to as many people as the message of biological warm-bloodedness reached out to many higher animal species? Will the new messenger ever be categorized with the *megazostrodons* and other early mammals (that looked like *mice* and *rats)* because he *has lived their lives, resembled their features* and *delivered their warm-blooded message to humans?* Time will tell.

PART TWO

THE NATURE OF INTERNATIONAL TRADE SPECIES

6

The Cold-Blooded Species

Economists often do disagree, but that has not been true with respect to international trade. Ever since Adam Smith there has been virtual unanimity among economists, whatever their ideological position on other issues, that international free trade is in the best interest of the trading countries and of the world. [1]

Milton Friedman

Expansion of Reptilian Species to Global Economies

As if the reptilian species—that horrify humans in wild life and in domestic economic policies—are not enough, humans have to confront more reptilian species in international trade theories and practices. The types of species dwelling in the habitats of international trade are the same as those in domestic economies. They too include three reptilian categories: 1) *cold-blooded species*, 2) *hibernating species*, and 3) *species of mixed cold-bloodedness and hibernation*. There is no single species either in academia or in actual trade policy in the entire world that can be classified as *warm-blooded* yet.

The question of which reptilian school of thought to follow in international trade is one of the oldest and most controversial arguments in economics. The arguments of the pros and cons of each of these reptilian schools of thoughts are enormous. In academia, they have filled many textbooks, economical journals, post-graduate and doctoral theses. They have also been the subject of economic research.

In all discussions about international trade, the pros and cons try to exaggerate the advantages of their favored reptilian species and denounce others. The assumptions behind their theories and arguments are unrealistic and have little to do with the real world. Most arguments are semi-emotional and often loaded with deceptions ranging from half-truths to outright falsehood.

Such intellectual abuse cannot go on forever. We need a completely different way of thinking. We need something that is objective, logical and fair in classifying species of international trade. A biological analogy in which we compare trade species with biological species should fill such a need. It takes a little sophistication for an average person with simple common sense to understand the advantages and disadvantages of cold-bloodedness, hibernation and warm-bloodedness in animals, and which to select, if there was a choice. It should not take more sophistication to understand their counterparts in international trade.

The Logic of Cold-Bloodedness

We have seen in earlier chapters that laissez-faire capitalism is an extension of the philosophy of reptilian cold-bloodedness to domestic economies. *Free trade* is another extension of the same philosophy to the world of international trade. Such a system is also called *open economy* or *cold-blooded reptilian trade*. Like all other applications of reptilian cold-bloodedness, free trade means that all kinds of trade control, such as tariffs, quotas, subsidies or voluntary export restriction, should be entirely eliminated. Advocates of free trade call all methods of control trade barriers. They argue that all these barriers should be removed and governments should not discriminate against import or interfere with export.

In free trade systems, consumers and firms use discretion options to satisfy their selfish interest the same way cold-blooded reptiles use discretion options to regulate their blood temperature. There is a significant difference, though. Reptiles intentionally use discretion options to stabilize their blood temperature. Individuals and firms are different. They look at their selfish needs and do not care about the overall economic picture. Advocates of free trade claim this tendency is not a problem and should not make cold-bloodedness in free trade much worse then cold-bloodedness in reptiles! They argue that when individuals and firms seek selfish interests, the overall prosperity of the society is enhanced as if there was an *invisible hand* that promotes such prosperity.

According to free trade doctrines, market forces and free competition between domestic and foreign products are preferable to government intervention. Free market forces will, in the long run, correct temporary distortions and inequities such as trade deficits and casualties of local industries and their workers that are threatened by free trade. Government intervention in trade issues constitute an abridgment of economic freedom. Once nations entrust economic life to free market mechanism, the invisible hand will bring about optimum results.

While pure cold-blooded biological systems may be found in many reptiles, and pure cold-blooded laissez-faire capitalism was practiced in the nineteenth century by Great Britain and the U.S., pure cold-bloodedness in trade is a concept rather than a fact. It is more theoretical than practical. Absolute free trade, in which all kinds of government control on export and import are entirely eliminated, does not exist anywhere. No country would dare to give it a try as it may causes immediate death of many local industries. The challenge for any nation interested in free trade is to find out that level of cold-bloodedness in which it can survive a reasonably long time before its industrial base goes extinct.

The theoretical case for free trade is based on the work of Adam Smith who also laid the intellectual foundation of laissez-faire capitalism. Smith argued that division of labor and specialization among countries is similar to the division of labor among individuals. The benefits nations receive through trade are essentially the same as that individuals receive. In both cases, specialization leads to greater efficiency and higher economic output.

David Ricardo, the English economist of the early nineteenth century, provided a more refined theory to prove the advantage of free trade. This theory is called the *principle of comparative advantage*. The theory holds that each nation should specialize in the production and export of the goods in which it has a comparative advantage over other countries. The comparative advantage is influenced by factors such as natural resources, cheap labor or skills. Then, the goods will be produced with greatest relative efficiency at low cost. Conversely, each country should import those goods in which they do not have a comparative advantage.

The major defect of the classical theory of comparative advantage lies in its oversimplified assumptions. The argument that trade between nations is similar to trade between individuals ignores complex issues of international trade such as trade deficits, importance of tariff revenue and erosion of industrial base. The claim that workers who lose their jobs in industries hurt by global competition will move to other high productivity jobs in export industries is too optimistic. The laid-off workers are more likely to end up in the service economy flipping hamburgers or behind cash registers. Also, the claimed increase in efficiency due to specialization among nations is exaggerated. Even specialization and division of labor in factories has received a slap in the face lately. The Japanese challenged this sacred theory and proved beyond doubt that cellular manufacturing is more productive and encourages more innovation by workers than typical assembly line specialization. Whether in labor or among nations, specialization is like everything in life. Too much is as bad as too little.

Because comparative advantage is a fancy theory with little application to the real world, it seems that only economists can understand it. Economists cling to the theory more strongly, as a kind of badge that defines their professional identity and ratifies their intellectual superiority. In fact, the statements "I understand the principle of comparative advantage," has become part of the economist's credo."[2] This explains why the vast majority of economists embrace free trade and why it has passionate defenders in academia.

Principles of Cold-Bloodedness

Cold-bloodedness in reptiles implies two main principles: 1) acceptance of excessive fluctuations in blood temperature and energy levels as a natural response to changes in external environment, and 2) cruelty and savageness.

Likewise, cold-bloodedness in free trade means huge fluctuations in figures of trade deficits, currency rates, output from domestic industries and rate of closing plants and moving jobs overseas are accepted as normal. Trade cold-bloodedness means cruelty and savageness as well. An industry that cannot face global competition ought to be killed off, along with its workers and their communities, by brutal competition from more efficient foreign industries. This Darwinian rationale for free trade sounds ruthless and cold-blooded indeed.

Which Species are Attracted the Most to Cold-Bloodedness?

Body size, both in absolute terms and relative to other competing species, is the most important factor in determining whether a reptilian species can survive with cold-bloodedness for a reasonably long geological time before it goes extinct. The minimum body size needed to survive under cold-bloodedness depends on the climate. If the climate is tropical and food sources are abundant, cold-blooded species will be able to survive even if their body size is relatively small. When the climate becomes seasonal, then body size can make a difference. Only larger species can survive tougher climates without the need for hibernation. The more seasonal and colder the climate, the bigger is the minimum size needed to survive with cold-bloodedness. In extremely harsh climates, size will not make any difference; all cold-blooded species die off, no matter how huge they are.

What is true about biological species is also true of trade systems. The size of a nation's economy, both in absolute terms and relative to other competing trade nations, is the most important factor in determining how well a nation survives with a free trade policy before its economic power goes extinct.

If the global economic climate is perfect and if every nation opens its trading doors fully, more nations will be able to survive under free trade, even if their economies are relatively small. As the climate of global competition becomes colder, then the size of the economy can make a difference. Only rich nations with huge economies can survive free trade without the need for protectionism. The tougher and more brutal the climate of global competition, the larger is the minimum size of the economy needed to survive free trade. In extremely harsh climates, the size of the economy will not be a major factor as all nations adopting free trade policies will find that their industrial base dies off, no matter how huge their economies are.

Because the climate of international trade is relatively colder than typical earth climates, only two nations in the entire Age of Reptilian Economics and Politics could afford to practice free trade. These nations are *nineteenth century Great Britain* and *post-World War II U.S.* All other nations had to live with protectionism of varying degrees. This pattern of reptilian behavior is peculiar. Unlike the Age of Reptiles when cold-bloodedness was the rule and hibernation was the exception, the Age of Reptilian Economics and Politics featured hibernation in trade as the rule and cold-bloodedness as the exception.

While the parallel between the two champions of free trade is dramatic, the parallel between both of them on one hand and the mighty dinosaurs on the other hand is even more striking. Both nations emerged as the richest and strongest economies in the world. Each became an overwhelming global power that dominated the earth's economic, political and military affairs. This makes them the closest in size and might to the gigantic dinosaurs.

But size is spoiling. In ideal conditions and in the absence of strong competitors, size deceives animals and nations. Size lets them not only survive on cold-bloodedness, but also to rise and dominate the planet for quite a long time. Dinosaurs ruled the planet for over two hundred million years during the Age of Reptiles. Great Britain and the U.S. enjoyed being a world power for over 120 years during the Age of Reptilian Economics and Politics.

Great Britain practiced and preached free trade for a period that stretched over seventy years. The British economists Adam Smith and David Ricardo both advocated free trade and established its intellectual foundation. In 1860, through the efforts of William Gladstone, then the chancellor of the exchequer, Great Britain became a free-trade country, keeping only a few small duties for revenue.

Great Britain continued to practice free trade throughout the nineteenth century and the beginning of the twentieth century, even after its economic power started to decline and became insufficient to support free trade. Continuing in cold-blooded trade policy was a matter of a habit; there was no motivation to change the cold-blooded reptilian habit unless a catastrophe happens.

It was the Ice Age of the Great Depression that forced Great Britain to abandon its free trade policy and retreat to protectionism. The combination of the Great Depression and a diminishing British dominance in the world economy led to a rise in anti-cold-bloodedness and pro-hibernation sentiment. In 1932, under intense pressure to end the unrealistic embrace of the free trade principle, Britain established a policy called imperial preferences. The new policy prescribed free trade only among members of the Commonwealth, excluding outsiders. After ruling for more than seventy years with a free trade policy, the mighty champion was brought to an end by the catastrophe of the Great Depression.

From 1932 until the end of World War II, no nation embraced free trade in the western world. After the war, the U.S. assumed the role of the leading advocate of reptilian cold-bloodedness in trade. It continued in this role throughout the second half of the twentieth century because it was by far the world's largest trading economy and the closest in size and power to nineteenth century Great Britain and gigantic dinosaurs.

The U.S. took a more positive step in promoting free trade than Great Britain. It led to the establishment of the GATT (General Agreement on Tariffs and Trade), aimed at reducing trade barriers. The U.S. used intense political pressure to persuade other countries to move in the direction of free trade and away from protectionism.

Because most nations fear the risks of free trade and prefer the safety of protectionism, free trade is not a viable situation unless imposed by a dominant country that has the power and muscles to intimidate other nations. There is a limit, though, on what U.S. pressure can do to force significant changes in trade policy abroad. Politicians in other countries answer primarily to domestic interests, just as we do. Many people and politicians in other countries are furious and defiant in the face of American pressure to push them toward free trade.

Despite the U.S. pressure, GATT negotiations resulted in little progress in the 1990s. The U.S., therefore, turned its attention in free trade toward its neighbors. It signed the North America Free Trade Agreement (NAFTA) with Canada and Mexico, which went into effect on January 1, 1994. All barriers on goods and services will be phased out. The agreement gave the three nations concerned limited exposure to free trade between themselves, but this did not extend to the rest of the world. The U.S. is still facing difficulties in persuading most countries of the virtues of free trade.

Another difficulty the U.S. is encountering is the decline of its economic power during the 1980s and early 1990s. This is a mirror image of the decline of Great Britain in the twentieth century and of the dinosaurs at the end of the Cretaceous Period. Despite the recent U.S. decline, manifested in the erosion of its industrial base and persistent trade deficit, the U.S. is determined to continue its free trade policy. As with Great Britain, it is a matter of a cold-blooded reptilian habit. After all, the U.S. can endure for quite some time the burdens that result from free trade policy, which would immediately crush other nations.

The question of why the U.S. throws its gigantic weight behind free trade is an interesting one. It bears directly on the central question of how cold-blooded ideology influences the present and future of cold-blooded reptilism in both domestic and world trade.

No matter how determined the U.S. is to continue its current free trade practices, these must end sooner or later. Great Britain had to make the hard choice of abandoning free trade and accepting protectionism in 1932. There has been a resurgence of similar protectionist pressure in recent years; the argument being that the U.S. cannot afford a free trade policy while the rest of the world practices protectionism. However, the U.S. does not have to follow Great Britain's footsteps in abandoning free trade and accepting protectionism. We are lucky to have another new choice: the *warm-blooded trade policy*. And switching from cold-bloodedness to warm-bloodedness in trade would not be shameful and disappointing, unlike retreating to hibernation.

When Does Cold-bloodedness Become Attractive?

The popularity of cold-bloodedness among animal species increases when the climates are tropical and ideal.

The same tendency is also applicable to trade species. The idea of free trade and the classical theory of comparative advantage retain their popularity and relevance only when economic conditions are ideal. The same idea and theory—along with the academic views of prestigious economists—are sold at large discounts when economic conditions are freezing cold.

The ideal condition for promoting free trade happened first to Great Britain. The end of the Napoleonic wars and the coming of the Industrial Revolution saw Great Britain emerge as the unchallenged leader among nations. The combination of factors such as the gigantic size of the British economy and the colonization of many nations—as sources of cheap raw material and markets for manufactured products—created a perfect climate. Such ideal conditions were enough to persuade the people to enjoy the status of a free trade nation and get rid of the dull practice of trade protectionism.

This ideal climate also occurred for the U.S. after World War II. The destruction of industrial capacity in Europe and Japan let the U.S. attain a similar position to that of Great Britain at the end of the Napoleonic wars. The lack of powerful competitors was spoiling. It allowed the U.S. to emerge as the unchallenged economic power. Even after competing nations recovered fully from the war destruction and after the U.S. lost its once-vaunted superiority over other nations in technology, things did not change. It found itself chained to the cold-blooded reptilian habit it had become used to during the prior period of ideal climate.

Apart from these two cases of perfect climate characterized by destruction of competing nations after major wars such as the

Napoleonic wars and World War II, the climate of trade is influenced by two main factors. The first factor is how open nations are to trade. When nations adopt either free or warm-blooded trade policy, the climate becomes warmer. Conversely, when nations retreat to protectionism and close their doors to imports, the climate gets colder, as happened during the Great Depression.

The second factor that affects the climate of trade is the spread of modern technology and industrialization to developing countries with abundant, cheap labor. This makes imports from these countries cheaper than domestic products, causing intensified competition and bringing a chill to global trade. This factor will continue to intensify, making the climate of global trade more freezing and more brutal every year.

What the U.S. trade policy and free trade proponents hope is that the warmth from opening trade and removing barriers will be greater than the chill caused by spreading technology to developing countries. Then more nations could be persuaded to switch from protectionism to free trade. But this scenario is just wishful thinking. Climate has never stayed ideal and tropical indefinitely, certainly not for the cold-blooded dinosaurs or for Great Britain. Why should it do so for a free trade nation like the U.S.?

Advantages of Cold-Bloodedness

If animals had something comparable to human intelligence during the Age of Reptiles, each species would ask itself, "What are the advantages and disadvantages that follow from adopting reptilian cold-bloodedness in terrestrial living? Would the animal kingdom be better off if all animals adhere strictly to cold-bloodedness all the time, or if they retreat to hibernation?"

To answer these questions, reptiles would hold debates in the jungles. On the right, pros of cold-bloodedness would brag about its advantages and how reptilian species achieved tremendous progress compared to fish and amphibian species, thanks to reptilian cold-bloodedness. On the left, the cons would raise all disadvantages and hardships that arise from cold-bloodedness. The debate might be interesting, but it would feature only part of the truth. The full truth would only be revealed when the animals recognize warm-bloodedness as a legitimate choice that should be fairly represented in the debate.

The pros of cold-bloodedness would point to three major advantages: increased freedom, efficiency and life enjoyment. They would argue that these advantages outweigh the side effects of increased vulnerability and hardships. Obviously the claimed advantages are only relative to hibernation.

The first advantage is that cold-blooded reptiles make all discretionary choices and are free from hibernation control. In addition, the cold-blooded reptilian system is the most efficient biological system in terms of the amount of food energy required to maintain full living. Most important, cold-blooded reptiles enjoy all functions of living and do not have to settle for the hibernation coma.

Humans can do things that animals did not have the chance to do. Economists ask themselves, "What are the economic gains and losses that follow from adopting free trade? Would countries be better off if they adhere strictly to free trade all the time, or if they retreat to protectionism?"

To answer these questions, there have been so many debates in the jungles of economic literature. On the right, advocates of free trade would brag about how global economies and international trade achieved tremendous progress, thanks to free trade. On the left, opponents would raise all the disadvantages and hardships that arise from cold-bloodedness in free trade, which are as awful as those of reptiles. The debate might be interesting, but it, too, features only a small part of the truth. The full truth will only be revealed when our economic and political system recognizes warm-blooded trade policy as a legitimate choice that should be fairly represented in the debate.

The supporters of free trade point to the same three major advantages of biological cold-bloodedness: increased freedom, efficiency and enjoyment of life. Obviously these claimed advantages are relative only to protectionism, not to warm-blooded trade policy. It is interesting, however, to see what goes on in the mind of the free-traders and see how it reflects a cold-blooded reptilian mentality.

As the name suggests, the first advantage of free trade is that it provides maximum freedom because government control in trade policy is minimized. Consumers have full freedom to buy imports or domestic products, whichever they prefer. Business executives are free to keep plants and jobs here or move them overseas and then import cheap products instead of manufacturing them at home. The government does not have to step on the backs of consumers and producers by influencing how they make their own decisions.

The second advantage is increased efficiency. The theory of comparative advantage attempts to prove the superior efficiency that results from specialization among nations. The reason is that free trade forces nations to let their relatively weak industries die off, and concentrate instead on producing goods in which they have relative advantages compared to foreign competitors. When all nations are committed to free trade, the world will get more output from its limited amounts of resources and a higher level of material well-being. Also, free trade promotes economies of scale as a result of specialization. The argument is that the larger the firm, the lower is the production cost per unit output. In addition, free trade promotes more global competition and deters domestic monopoly. The increased competition from abroad forces domestic firms to adopt lowest-cost production techniques. It also compels them to be innovative and progressive with respect to product quality and production methods, thereby contributing to economic growth.

The third advantage of free trade is increased life enjoyment. Free trade enables consumers to enjoy a wide range of options to satisfy all diversified tastes. Thanks to free trade, Americans today enjoy countless products from all over the world no protectionist country could match, even to a small degree. But the most important question is, how long we can enjoy the cold-blooded reptilian status in free trade before our economic power and industrial base go extinct?

Disadvantages of Cold-Bloodedness

Biological cold-bloodedness creates hardships and vulnerability for the affected animal species caught in a cold climate. When climate is excessively harsh, death and even extinction of the entire species will follow.

Free trade creates similar symptoms for the affected nations. Under free trade, local industries and their workers suffer the most as a result of unfair foreign competition. Cheap imports flood domestic markets and the prices of manufactured goods—along with jobs and wages of local workers—are pulled down. The symptoms of free trade vary from reduced wages and too many concessions of workers and unions to loss of jobs as plants are closed or moved overseas. The industries hurt by competition, their workers and the affected regions feel they are being singled out to carry the burden of progress so that consumers can feel good. The combination of shrinking employment in industries eroded by competition and lower wages reduces standards of living.

Another drawback of free trade is loss of tariff revenue for the federal government as a result of being too generous to imports. Today, income tax and social security tax are the main sources of revenue of the federal government. Although they have increased dramatically during the last three decades, we suffered from large budget deficits for all the 1980s and most of the 1990s. America needs to raise its tariff revenue and lower other taxes. During the period of trade protectionism that extended up to World War II, tariffs brought in about half of the U.S. government tax revenue.

A third drawback of free trade is trade deficits. A trade deficit means exports of goods and services do not pay for imports. This condition is considered unfavorable because the nation suffering from trade deficit must borrow from the rest of the world to finance that deficit. The failure to "pay the way" in international trade is usually interpreted as a sign of domestic weakness: the nation consumes more than it produces. Although trade deficit is a serious problem, it is not blamed as often as budget deficit.

As a result of moving aggressively toward free trade in an increasingly cold global environment, the U.S. experienced very large and persistent trade deficits throughout the 1980s and 1990s. In 1985, the U.S. status changed from that of a net creditor nation to that of a debtor nation for the first time in seventy years. Not only must we borrow from the rest of the world in order to finance the trade deficit, but we also need to sell American assets. Payment to foreigners either in terms of interest on loans or dividends on assets will continue to be a drain on our resources. The longer the present free trade continues, the larger this drain will become.

Foreign borrowing and selling of American assets are essentially a way to help live several years or probably a few decades more with free trade. This will be at the expense of saddling future generations—even when they decide to switch to a warm-blooded trade policy—with the burden of paying current bills.

Americans have become relaxed about trade deficit, foreign borrowing and selling assets because these cold-blooded symptoms of free trade have continued so long that it seems as if they can do so forever. A key reason for this relaxed attitude is that American assets are huge, like gigantic dinosaurs. America has about than $60,000 billion of private assets. If the trade deficit continues at an average $150 billion in present dollars, it will take America about 400 years to sell virtually everything to foreigners. We can live, therefore, with free trade much longer than most people think. Dinosaurs were in a similar situation and lived with cold-bloodedness for two hundred million years. While our situation is not cause for immediate panic, it should be taken seriously. An unexpected catastrophe like the one that wiped out dinosaurs at the end of the Cretaceous Period may happen to us, too. Our own catastrophe will be triggered when the confidence of foreign investors is shaken and they decide to withdraw their money, causing a crash in our financial markets.

In spite of the huge and horrifying risks of free trade, the U.S. has decided to live with it and follow the footsteps of nineteenth century Great Britain and the gigantic dinosaurs. The U.S. has no interest in changing its trade policy as this would require abandoning cold-bloodedness in trade and switching to either hibernation or warm-bloodedness. That is something the U.S. would not do unless it came face to face with freezing economic environment triggered by a sudden financial crises!

Weighing Advantages and Disadvantages

In the absence of the warm-blooded choice, the advantages of biological cold-bloodedness would seem plausible. The disadvantages would sound serious, but animals may live with them. With hindsight regarding what the warm-blooded did for mammals and birds, the picture will turn completely upside down.

The three claimed advantages of cold-bloodedness—freedom, efficiency and life enjoyment—are deceptive when we compare cold-blooded reptiles with warm-blooded birds and mammals. While cold-blooded reptiles are freed from the control of blood temperature and energy levels, this freedom does not mean much. Because reptiles have to worry constantly about how and if they can make their blood temperature reach a reasonable level, they do not have much freedom to do things they want to do. The claimed advantage of efficiency is illusive. Reptiles are at a disadvantage in earning their food because of their cold-bloodedness and sluggishness. And warm-blooded animals should enjoy their life more than cold-blooded reptiles. So not only are these advantages deceptive, but the disadvantages and the risks of extinction through catastrophe are more than they seem.

So it is that in the absence of warm-blooded trade policy, the advantages of free trade seem reasonable and plausible. The disadvantages may sound horrifying to some of us, but we can live with them for quite some time. The picture will change dramatically in the minds of the next generations when they will experience what warm-blooded trade policy can do.

Our children will see more evidence proving that the three claimed advantages of free trade systems are as deceptive as those of cold-blooded reptilian systems. While our economy is free to a great extent from government control on trade policy, this form of freedom does not mean much. We are selling American assets at a high rate to live with large and persistent trade deficits. Growing foreign ownership of American assets compromises our national sovereignty and erodes our independence both political and economic. We have merely replaced government control on trade with increasing foreign control over our economic assets.

The claimed advantage of increased efficiency in free trade is also deceptive. The simplistic definition of efficiency refers to cheaper imports. But look at the price we pay: We are eroding our industrial base, forcing many manufacturing plants into extinction, lowering the wages of our workers, selling our assets, and depriving the government of significant tariff revenue so that we can enjoy some kind of deceptive efficiency. We have to distinguish between apparent and true efficiency. The latter includes all the hidden cost of free trade.

The third claimed advantage, of increased enjoyment of consumers, as they can buy anything from everywhere in the world is illusive. We live with continuous worry about trade deficit, jobs for our children and increased foreign ownership.

If the advantages of free trade are deceptive and illusory, and the possibilities of economic extinction are great and serious, why do most economists endorse free trade? The answer is *symbolism* and *pride*. Cold-bloodedness in free trade is a *symbol* of cold-blooded capitalism and cold-blooded reptilism. And humans seem to take *pride* in belonging mentally to *class reptilia* in their trade, economic and political systems!

7
The Hibernating Species

Most people want security in this world, not liberty.
                                        Henery L. Mencken (1956)

The Logic of Hibernation

Hibernation is the opposite of cold-bloodedness. This means that hibernation replaces lack of control of blood temperature and energy levels with excessive and rigid control on these biological functions. The intensity of hibernation control is so high that the animal gives up consciousness and sense of living. It has to isolate itself from the cold environment in a den or a ground hole, reduce its biological activities and hide until the cold season is over. Hibernation is regarded as a last resource option. This means when cold-bloodedness works for a certain reptilian species, it should be preferable to hibernation. But when cold-bloodedness is not adequate for preserving life, animals must be prepared to accept the hibernation coma rather than face death.

It will be abundantly clear to the reader that while free trade extends the principle of reptilian cold-bloodedness to the world of trade, protectionism extends the principle of hibernation. Whether one looks at trade systems directly or in the light of the biological analogy, protectionism is the opposite of free trade. It replaces the "no government control" status of free trade with excessive and rigid government control. The intensity of protectionism control is so high that people give up free choices. They have to reduce their consumption of foreign products and accept lower living standards. These sacrifices are the price nations pay to isolate and protect their domestic industries from foreign competition.

Like biological hibernation, protectionism is generally regarded as a last resource option. This means when free trade works, it should be preferable to protectionism. But when free trade is not adequate, nations must be prepared to accept a hibernating lifestyle of protectionism rather than face the extinction of their industrial base. Fear of death and extinction is more horrifying than fear of being haunted by the ghosts of Adam Smith and David Ricardo for violating their sacred teachings and commands.

Means of Hibernation

Hibernation in animals takes a typical form. First, the hibernator builds up fat reserve in its body to prepare for the cold season. Most hibernators dig holes in the ground as shelters. Big hibernators may retreat to caves or dens. The shelter isolates the hibernator from the surroundings. Once the animal retreats to the shelter, it goes into a coma in which it reduces its breathing, heartbeat, metabolism and feeding to the minimum level needed to barely sustain life.

While human hibernation in international trade is reasonably similar to animal hibernation in principle and objective, it has a few differences. Humans skip the preparation phase of building up fat reserve before the hibernation session. The main reason is that most humans think more about the present and do not care about the future. Another reason is that humans are too proud to learn from animals. Also, hibernation in trade should be continuous, at least for several generations with no awakening interruptions. With continuous hibernation, there is no time for the preparation phase.

The means of trade hibernation are also unique to the human species. Unlike animals which have more or less the same way of hibernation, trade hibernation has more varieties and is more colorful, thanks to human creativity.

The first and oldest means of trade hibernation is *tariffs*. Tariffs are like federal sales tax, but imposed only on imports. By increasing the price of imports, tariffs encourage consumers to buy more domestic and less foreign products. Economists classify tariffs into two kinds, in terms of their hibernation effectiveness: *prohibitive* and *revenue* tariffs. A prohibitive tariff is one that is so high as to completely discourage imports and thus shield domestic producers from foreign competition. Revenue tariff, on the other hand, provides federal government with tax revenue. To achieve such a goal, it has to allow a relatively larger volume of imports. Thus revenue tariffs are not as high as prohibitive tariffs. An implication, therefore, is that a good revenue tariff provides little hibernation protection, and a good prohibitive tariff provides little revenue to the government. Because of the relatively lower protection provided by revenue tariffs, debates over protectionist trade policy usually center on prohibitive tariffs.

The second means of trade hibernation is *quotas*. By limiting the quantity of imports, quotas are more effective in retarding imports and providing deeper levels of hibernation than tariffs. The reason is that a given product might be imported in relatively large quantities despite tariffs, while import quotas, on the other hand, completely prohibit imports once quotas are filled. There is a price paid for this deeper level of hibernation. Tariffs at least provide revenue to the government, but import quotas provide nothing. The windfall price increase from quotas accrues to the importer who is lucky or influential enough (or sufficiently generous enough with favors and bribes) to get an import license.

Voluntary export restriction is a relatively new means of protectionism that exactly resembles quotas in limiting the quantity of imports and in providing a deeper level of trade hibernation. The only minor difference is that the restrictions are imposed by the exporting country instead of the importing country. A good example is when Japanese auto manufacturers agreed to voluntary export restrictions to the U.S. in 1980. Voluntary export restrictions are not really as voluntary as the name suggests. The U.S., for example, put political pressure on Japan to limit its auto exports. The Japanese knew that if they did not impose voluntary restrictions on Japanese cars, Congress would enforce mandatory ones. Faced with this threat, the Japanese yielded to the pressure and agreed to voluntary restrictions.

The main advantage of voluntary export restrictions is that the importing country can pretend that it is not practicing protectionism. Like the case of the U.S., it can point its finger to the Japanese for volunteering to do the sinful hibernation practice for them. This situation is like a person who is too ashamed and feels too guilty to steal something. To solve his problem, he harasses another person to steal for him. Since he does not commit the act directly, he can convince himself that he should assume no moral responsibility for it. He can point his finger at the other person and claim that the individual has just volunteered to do the act for him.

Another trade hibernation method that is more direct than the so-called voluntary export restriction is *export subsidies.* The objective of the subsidies is to allow the exporting industries to sell their products for less overseas. Such subsidies may take the form of outright cash disbursements, exemptions, preferential financing or other preferential treatment for exports. Throughout the 1980s, many nations subsidized their computer industries, and European governments continued to subsidize the multinational Airbus Industrie Consortium. In these days of horrendous budget deficits, the worst side effect of export subsidies is that they can cost governments a lot of money.

Other trade hibernation means are indirect. They include complex import licensing requirements and unreasonable standards pertaining to product quality and safety, and simply unnecessary bureaucratic red tape in custom procedures. Japan and many European countries require import firms to obtain licenses. By restricting the issuance of licenses, imports can be effectively restricted.

The great majority of economists condemn all methods of trade hibernation as much as strict religious leaders condemn sin, but cannot give clear answers on how to avoid it completely. When there is an urgent need for a nation to hibernate behind protectionist walls and the pressure is too hard to resist, economists advise the hibernating nation to select revenue tariffs as the least sinful option. The main advantage of tariffs is that they are simple, clear, easy to administer, and also provide ample revenue for governments strapped by budget deficits. Then we can get something a bit righteous out of the different sinful means of practicing hibernation in trade.

Which Species Are Attracted the Most to Hibernation?

Little and vulnerable animals seek hibernation protection during cold seasons. Without hibernation, their bodies lose a lot of heat to their surroundings, and they die.

Likewise, small and vulnerable nations are attracted the most to trade protectionism. Without hibernating trade policy, their industrial base loses most of its customers to competing foreign firms, and their domestic industries eventually die off.

Because the climate of international trade is extremely cold, the great majority of nations find themselves vulnerable to foreign competition and therefore seek protectionism. As we have seen, the only two exceptions to this have been nineteenth century Great Britain and post-World War II U.S. All other nations practice trade protectionism to varying degrees. The smaller the size of the economy and the lower the living standard, the deeper the level of protectionism the nation seeks.

The U.S. is a good example of how a nation can evolve from a hibernating status to a cold-blooded status in trade as the size of its economy grows. Throughout most of its history up to the end of World War II, the U.S. was a protectionist country with tariffs reaching as high as 70 percent of import values. High tariffs had popular support, especially among Republicans. Most people felt that it would be tough to face foreign competition, especially from European countries that were more advanced in industry and technology at that time.

The end of World War II turned the hibernating status of the U.S. upside down. The industrial base of competing European countries and Japan was destroyed. The U.S. emerged as the most powerful economy in the world. With a relatively large economic size and an ideal climate, it found itself no longer needing protectionism. It was more logical, therefore, to abandon hibernation and evolve into a cold-blooded trade nation.

Today, the developing countries are passing through the hibernating stage the U.S. went through during the nineteenth century and the first half of the twentieth century. Most of these countries are in even more vulnerable condition. They definitely need the safety of protectionism. Hibernation in trade is as understandable from nations with vulnerable economies as it is expected from small animal species. What is not understandable and not expected are the hibernation practices sought by nations of large, developed economies like Japan, Western European countries and Canada. These nations could afford to survive for some time as respectable cold-blooded trade nations like the U.S. They simply do not have the courage to pursue cold-bloodedness and abandon their defensive hibernation practices!

When Does Hibernation Become Attractive?

The popularity of hibernation among animal species peaks when the climates are freezing and food supplies are scarce, such as in geological ice ages.

So it is that protectionist ideas and practices become attractive among voters and successful politicians in economic ice ages, namely periods of severe recessions and depressions.

The freezing conditions are as intimidating to people as to animals. Under such conditions, ordinary people simply do not listen to the warnings of economists to resist the natural tendency to hibernate through protectionism and to stick instead to free trade. They throw such advice, along with the teachings of Adam Smith and David Ricardo, into the garbage cans provided in election campaigns. As uninformed people ignore the advice of experts, they find themselves committing hibernation sins one after the other.

The most unforgivable hibernation sin was committed in 1930, when Congress passed the *Smoot-Hawley Hibernation Act*, which imposed the highest tariff increases ever enacted in U.S. history. Thanks to the act, average tariff rates reached 60 percent (compared to 5 percent now). The distinguished Senators who voted for the hibernation act and President Hoover who approved it thought trade hibernation should be similar to biological hibernation. Trade hibernation would likely provide similar protection at the price of temporary lower consumption of foreign goods and other inconvenient sacrifices such as lowered living standards. Since the Great Depression was an extremely cold ice age, they sought the deepest hibernation levels. They had no idea that they were conducting the most horrifying hibernation experiments ever done on the human species in the history of international trade.

The Smoot-Hawley Act experiment showed an interesting and unique phenomenon in trade hibernation that never happens in animal hibernation. In trade hibernation, there is a very delicate ecological balance between the increase in hibernation participation among trading nations and the temperature of the international trade environment. Once the balance is altered by a large, sudden hibernation move like that caused by the Smoot-Hawley Act, things will get out of control.

Tampering with the ecological balance in trade may be done for sound hibernation reasons with no intention to do any harm, but it may cause horrible consequences. When a nation increases the depth of its trade hibernation it actually lowers the temperature of the trade environment. The hibernating nation tries to promote the survival of its domestic industries by exporting unemployment and chilliness to foreign trading partners. The sad truth is that the other trading partners respond to the increased chilliness by increasing their hibernation rate. This causes the temperature of the trade environment for the first nation to drop. Then it responds by increasing its hibernation even more. The situation is like the chain reaction of a nuclear blast, but instead of causing intense heat it generates unbearably freezing conditions to every nation.

Professional economists were aware of this scenario. They predicted that the Smoot-Hawley Act would deepen the Great Depression. Almost every American economist opposed the act.

If the majority of economists were against hibernation in trade, why did the Republican Congress and President Hoover support it? The answer lies in the psychology of fear and the threat of further economic decline. These factors overwhelm nations as much as severe ice ages overwhelm animals. In addition, the public was uninformed that trade hibernation is much worse and more risky than biological hibernation because of the extremely delicate ecological balance that is unique to trade. They had no idea that the hibernation act would tamper with the balance, resulting not only in increased hardship for the U.S., but global freezing conditions as well.

Once the hibernation act was put into effect, foreign countries found their export industries hurt because of the colder trade environment. Each nation responded by deepening its trade hibernation level, which caused the temperature of the trade environment to sink close to absolute zero, thus exacerbating that period's economic distress. Because of this cause-and-effect relationship, some economic scholars hold the Smoot-Hawley Act as partly responsible for the Great Depression. Others claim that the act forced Great Britain to abandon its free trade policy it had been practicing for over seventy years. Great Britain, the only champion of free trade at that time, had to retreat to protectionism in 1932 and give up free trade.

Proponents of free trade policy delight in telling the story of the Smoot-Hawley Hibernation Act over and over again. They hope that by showing trade hibernation is more risky than animal hibernation it will support their arguments for the need to adhere to cold-blooded free trade policy. Obviously no sensible person would like to be associated with something that has an everlasting terrible memory like the Smoot-Hawley Act and its hibernation team, which included Republican Representative Willis Hawley of Oregon and Senator Reed Smoot of Utah along with President Herbert Hoover. These three politicians entered History's Hall of Fame and earned the immortal status of being big fools in the eyes of all generations, thanks to their strong belief in trade hibernation.

In spite of the terrible legacy of the Smoot-Hawley Hibernation Act, there has been a recent resurgence of protectionism, especially during periods of economic hardship. The call for hibernation in trade is still heard when any domestic industry feels threatened by brutal global competition. The persistent trade deficits, feeds protectionist pressure even more.

The worst possible nightmare would be that the accumulation of such hibernation pressure may reach dangerous levels. Since the intensified pressure cannot be sustained forever, it is likely to burst in a replay of the Smoot-Hawley Act. So will begin another worldwide trade hibernation frenzy. After all, there is no logic and no learning from past experience in economics and politics, especially when global conditions suddenly become freezing cold and financial death is approaching fast.

Advantages of Hibernation

The main advantage of hibernation is that it preserves life and the future survival of animal species when external conditions are hostile, especially if such species are not that strong or large.

Proponents of protectionism claim that trade hibernation provides similar advantage to biological hibernation. Protectionism preserves local industries in the face of hostile global competition, especially when such industries are not that strong, efficient or do not have the economics of large-scale production. Protectionism saves jobs, reduces unemployment and enhances the survival of communities depending on such industries. The weaker the domestic industries, the more trade hibernation benefits the economy would receive.

Protectionists argue that the failure of the Smoot-Hawley Hibernation Act in 1930 is more of an exception than the general rule in trade hibernation. No matter how much damage it caused and how terrible it looked, it was just one incident. We cannot judge protectionism simply on one failure. Many nations repeatedly, smoothly and safely practiced trade hibernation, giving them some benefits. Trade hibernation, therefore, should be well-suited to as many nations as biological hibernation is to many animal species.

Protectionism is particularly needed for infant industries. A temporary shielding from the brutal global competition of more efficient foreign producers gives infant industry a chance to survive the initial stage, establish itself and become a more efficient producer. Without hibernation protection, infant industries would not be able to weather the initial stage of start-up and experimentation. But the special needs of infant industries are not an excuse for permanent trade hibernation. Infant industries are supposed to grow up, become stronger and eventually be able to face a cold environment with little hibernation protection.

Infant industries are not the only species vulnerable to a hostile trade environment. Mature and developed industries may face survival problems as well. Occasionally, there are periods of freezing conditions created by foreign producers *dumping* their goods onto American markets at prices below their average cost or at a price lower than in the home market. The foreign producers know that they can tamper with the temperature of the trade environment and are likely to get away with it. The objective of such a practice is to force American producers to go extinct, obtain monopoly power and then raise prices. The Japanese are the masters of this weapon. They used it successfully to drive out some American firms in computer chip and steel industries.

Because dumping is a legitimate reason for trade hibernation, it is prohibited under American trade law. When dumping occurs and it is shown to have hurt American firms, the federal government takes protectionist actions by imposing tariffs called "anti-dumping duties" on the dumped goods. Unfortunately such actions usually come too late, after fatal casualties have occurred in the victimized industries.

In addition to offsetting dumping, protectionism offsets other unfair practices that creates freezing conditions in trade competition, such as support subsidies and lower wages of many foreign manufacturers. The argument for protection, gauged to appeal to workers and labor unions, says, "How can American workers possibly compete with goods produced cheaply by foreign labor and subsidized by foreign governments? We need trade protection so that we can survive."

Another important motivation for protectionism is increased self-sufficiency. The argument is that trade protection helps to preserve or strengthen industries producing goods and material essential for domestic economy, and prevents too much dependence on foreign producers. The threat of increased vulnerability in wars from too much dependence on foreign goods has motivated countries to establish more protection for industries they deem essential for self-sufficiency and survival.

While the goal of self-sufficiency is impossible to obtain even with the deepest level of trade hibernation, a more realistic goal is increased economic diversification. Unlike free trade which encourages nations to specialize in the too few industries in which they enjoy comparative advantage, protectionism looks for more diversification. With more diversification and less specialization, protectionism helps nations avoid the risks of having too many of its eggs in a single basket.

Another advantage of protectionism is increasing revenue for federal governments which would help to decrease other taxes or reduce budget deficits. Also, protectionism should help in reducing trade deficits associated with the practice of free trade policy.

The numerous advantages that trade hibernation promises are too hard to ignore, especially when the cold-blooded symptoms of free trade in a hostile, global environment are too serious, too painful and too persistent.

Disadvantages of Hibernation

There is a huge price to be paid in return for acquiring the advantages of hibernation. Hibernating animals must endure miserable side effects. After all, nothing comes for nothing. During hibernation, animals sacrifice the joy and awareness of living. They have to settle for a coma in which all biological functions such as breathing, heartbeat, feeding and metabolism are reduced to minimum.

The price nations pay for the advantages of protectionism is similar. Protectionist nations must sacrifice their living standards, income and consumption of foreign goods. They have to settle for a trade coma in which exports and imports and interaction with other nations are highly reduced.

The first side effects of protectionism happen to consumers. Trade barriers increase the price of imports. Prices of domestic goods are likely to increase too because of lack of foreign competition. An increase in the price of goods lowers the purchasing power of consumers. In protectionist policy, consumers suffer so that workers of protected industries can feel good.

The second side effect is allowing inefficient, weak industries to survive by shielding them from global competition. Without competition, industries have little need to become more efficient.

Protectionism blocks the mutually beneficial process by which nations specialize in producing goods for which their knowledge and resources suit them. It promotes the expansion of relatively inefficient industries which do not have comparative advantage. The inefficient industries crowd out the relatively efficient ones and redirect the flow of skills and investment away from them.

In addition to allowing weak industries to survive and promoting domestic monopoly, protectionism allows labor unions to survive and demand more wages and rights for the workers. Critics of protectionism argue that it is unfair to let weaker species multiply and prosper—they should have been allowed to go under. Trade hibernation inhibits the extinction process that takes place naturally through foreign competition, by which inefficient industries go out of business and unneeded workers are laid off, thus making room for more efficient ones.

A less controversial issue of protectionism is that nations must deal with the problem of isolation. Hibernating nations assume the same lifestyle as hibernating animals. They must be isolated in their hiding places and lose contact with the outside world. This involves giving up the cultural and technological intermixing with other nations that result from trade.

No matter how awful the side effects of trade hibernation, humans can still live with them the same way some animal species live with biological hibernation. What nations cannot afford to face is the possibility of trade war as a result of a sudden, large hibernation move like the Smoot-Hawley Act of 1930. Instead of delivering protection to American firms, it deepened the Great Depression and caused more extinction casualties. Hibernating animals are luckier as their hibernation does not cause any harm to the delicate ecological balance. Only humans have to endure more risky ways of hibernation!

Weighing Advantages and Disadvantages

In the absence of the warm-blooded option, there is no chance for smaller species to survive the cold season other than through hibernation. The practice of hibernation must be boring and disgusting. Hibernating days should not be counted as part of the real lives of animals. However, if animals have to choose between hibernation and death, the choice of hibernation makes more sense.

Humans face a similar dilemma. In the absence of warm-blooded trade policy, there is no other way that small or developing economies can survive the hostile environment of global competition other than through hibernating protectionism. The hibernating practice of protectionism should be more boring and disgusting to humans than animals. The years nations spend under protectionism must be discounted from their lives. However, most nations are likely to endure the misery of hibernation in trade than watching their industrial base die off. That is why *humans join animals in accepting the depressing lifestyle of hibernation!*

8
The Mixed Species

The good things of life are not to be had singly, but
come to us with a mixture.

Charles Lamb (1833)

There Are More Species

In our economic and political systems, we have the freedom to
choose. That is the definition of democracy. Every American is
proud of such freedom. Unfortunately, the current choices in
international trade offered to people are limited to cold-bloodedness
and hibernation.

If you do not like cold-bloodedness, you can vote for politicians
promoting hibernation. If you do not like hibernation, you can
vote for politicians promoting cold-bloodedness. If you like
neither of them and feel both reptilian choices are an insult to
your intelligence, you do not have to participate in elections at all.
You can just stay home swallowing your outrage, wondering
why economists and politicians treat humans with less respect
than nature treats wild animals.

When our economists and politicians tell us that the choices in
trade are limited to free trade and protectionism, they are talking
nonsense. There are two more choices in trade policy: 1) mixing

cold-bloodedness of free trade with hibernation of protectionism, and 2) warm-blooded trade policies.

The Logic of Mixing Cold-Bloodedness and Hibernation

The mix between cold-bloodedness and hibernation has two types: intensity and seasonal. Intensity mix means hibernation intensity is reduced from deep hibernation to either moderate or drowsy hibernation. Seasonal mix means the animal sticks to cold-bloodedness as long as the climate is warm or hot. It switches to hibernation when the climate is cold.

Why would animals mix cold-bloodedness and hibernation? Why not just stick to either pure cold-bloodedness or continuous deep hibernation all the time? The answer is that survival forces animals to alternate and compromise between these two choices.

The rationale for mixing cold-bloodedness and hibernation in trade policies is basically the same as in animals. There is no logical reason that designs of trade systems should be limited to purely free trade or deep protectionism. There are infinite grades of mixing cold-bloodedness of free trade and hibernation of protectionism. There is no label yet for the mixed designs. Until economists and politicians come up with a proper label, we may call such systems *mixed cold-bloodedness/hibernation* trade systems, or *mixed free/protectionist* trade systems. People with a scientific background would be comfortable with the first label, while others may prefer the second one.

The mix between cold-bloodedness and hibernation in trade has two types: intensity and seasonal. Intensity mix means varying the intensity of government control on imports such as tariffs and quotas. In this way, the level of government control on trade may be varied to cause deep, moderate or drowsy hibernation. Seasonal mix means the people have the right to stick to free trade for as long as the climate of the trade environment allows them to do so. They can switch to protectionism when the economic climate is freezing cold. The seasonal mix is allowed only in countries with political freedom.

Another kind of mix is to apply cold-bloodedness in domestic economic policies and hibernation in trade at the same time. This kind of *split-personality* happened throughout most of the history of the Republican and Democratic Parties. Before World War II, the Republicans were leaning toward diminished government control over domestic economies. At the same time, they wanted a larger government role in trade. Republican politicians endorsed the Smoot-Hawley Hibernation Act in 1930. Biologically speaking, they believed in cold-blooded policies for domestic economies and in hibernating policies for international trade. At the same time, Democrats were leaning toward more hibernation in domestic economies and more cold-bloodedness in international trade.

This mental disease of *split-personality* persisted in the Republican and Democratic Parties from their earliest days until World War II. After the war, both Republicans and Democrats were cured of the split-personality syndrome. Republicans became believers in cold-bloodedness in policies of both domestic economies and trade. Democrats also moved more in the direction of more hibernation in trade so that it would be consistent with their hibernation style in economic policies.

The trend of Democrats supporting hibernation in domestic economies and international trade was interrupted by the Clinton administration. President Clinton had some hibernation tendencies when he spoke of international trade in the 1992 election campaign. But after the election, he became more attracted to cold-bloodedness and moved more aggressively in that direction than any Democratic president in history. Clinton may excuse himself by saying that he had to compromise with the cold-blooded Republican-controlled Congress. But at present, it is hard to distinguish between the cold-bloodedness of President Clinton and the cold-bloodedness of typical Republicans in trade issues.

Apart from Clinton's reasoning, why would humans mix cold-bloodedness of free trade with hibernation of protectionism? Humans have the same logical reasons as reptiles that mix cold-bloodedness and hibernation. Economic Survival forces humans to compromise between cold-bloodedness of free trade and hibernation of protectionism, even if they do not admit it.

Which Species Are Attracted to Mixing Cold-Bloodedness and Hibernation?

If we exclude animal species equipped with purely cold-blooded biological systems which never hibernate, then all other species within the reptile class fall under the category of mixed cold-blooded/hibernation systems.

Humans are somewhat different from animals in this category. Mixed cold-blooded/hibernation systems have more participation among trade species. There has never been a single trade system in history that can be accurately classified as a purely free trade system in which all kinds of government control on imports are entirely eliminated. There will never be one. All trade systems have some mix of cold-bloodedness of free trade and hibernation of protectionism.

While mixing free trade and protectionism in trade is the rule, such a mix is not recognized in economic literature or in political speeches. It is a pity that humans deny such a mix in spite of the fact that they use it more than reptiles!

When Will Mixed Species Be Recognized?

If reptiles were given a chance to describe their blood temperature and energy systems, they would have no problem admitting that most of their species apply a mix of cold-bloodedness and hibernation.

Humans are not as straightforward as animals; they have an ego problem. Economists and politicians classify trade systems as either free trade or protectionism simply because they like illusion and deception to comfort themselves or to fool others to follow their economic and political doctrines.

Will humans ever acknowledge the reality and recognize the practice of mixing cold-bloodedness of free trade with hibernation of protectionism? Probably not, unless a drastic change happens. As long as reptilian species rule in the world of economics, politics and trade, deception will continue. There is hope, however, that the analogy between animal species and trade species will help us open our eyes to recognize things that we currently deny their existence.

Advantages of Mixed Species

Cold-bloodedness has a reasonably good score compared to hibernation when it comes to an animal's freedom, biological activities and enjoyment of life. But cold-bloodedness fails in preserving life for small species in a cold environment. On the other hand, hibernation has a pretty good score in preserving life in a cold environment, but it fails in the area of the animal's freedom, biological activities and life enjoyment.

Mixing cold-bloodedness with hibernation in the biological designs of reptiles means giving up some of the impressive score in one area to achieve a passing score in other areas that need improvement. Nature has the same stringent requirements for passing survival tests as the best schools and colleges. Passing some courses with an impressive score is not an excuse for failing others, even if the average score is pretty good. The rationale of mixed designs is to achieve passing scores in every major area, even at the cost of lowering the favorable scores.

What is true for biological systems is also true for trade systems. Achieving a passing score in all major areas may be obtained by the proper mixing of cold-bloodedness of free trade with hibernation of protectionism. There is no fundamental difference between what reptiles do in their biological systems and what humans do in their trade systems.

While free trade has a reasonably good score in the area of freedom, economic activities and enjoyment of life for consumers, it fails in protecting the industrial base and in balancing trade. On the other hand, protectionism has a reasonably good score in protecting the industrial base and achieving trade surplus, provided that it does not reach such a deep hibernation level as the Smoot-Hawley Act. However, protectionism fails in terms of freedom for firms and individuals, economic output and enjoyment of life.

The philosophy of mixing free trade with protectionism is to sacrifice the high scores both free trade and protectionist systems achieve in certain areas, to just barely pass in the areas that otherwise would fail. The reason for such a compromise is that our standards in trade systems should be as strict as the standards for kids in schools and animals in nature. The proponents of mixed cold-bloodedness/hibernation systems feel good because theirs is the only system that passes in every major area. Every other system fails badly in something.

Disadvantages of Mixed Species

There are no real disadvantages for reptiles to mix cold-bloodedness with hibernation. In fact, these mixed biological designs can provide reptiles with a better survival chance in their environment.

Humans are not as practical as reptiles! They think that looking at trade systems as a mix of free trade and protectionism would add more complexity and more controversy. For instance, one may estimate that the U.S. trade system is 80 percent cold-blooded, 20 percent hibernating and 0 percent warm-blooded. Another person may look at it differently, saying it should be 90 percent cold-blooded, 10 percent hibernating and 0 percent warm-blooded. Critics of the mixed cold-bloodedness/hibernation concept argue that we already have enough controversies and confusion in trade theories and we do not need more.

To avoid controversial discussions, economists and politicians like to simplify and idealize things at the expense of distorting the reality. They would classify any trade system that is more than 50 percent cold-blooded as a free trade system. By the same token, any system that has more than 50 percent hibernation should be labeled a protectionist system. Most people have no patience for sophistication and mathematical calculations.

Another factor behind this reluctance is the vagueness and ambiguity of the concept of mixing free trade with protectionism. People like to have a clear identity and purpose. Unlike animals that care only about results, humans care more about philosophy and principles.

A third disadvantage of mixed systems is that they are dull. Free trade may be seen as exciting because it values freedom; protectionism because it appears to provide security. But a trade system with a mix of free trade and protectionism lacks the excitement voters look for during election campaigns. Successful politicians know that. Therefore, they never talk about mixed trade systems, although all current trade systems fall into this category.

Because of these reasons, economists do not recognize the concept of mixing cold-bloodedness of free trade with hibernation of protectionism in their literature. Whether the mixed systems are recognized or not, they do exist in the real world. By acknowledging and understanding these mixed systems, humans can know where they are in the evolution of their reptilian trade systems and how they can move toward warm-bloodedness and mammalism.

9

Abandoning Reptilism and Seeking Warm-Bloodedness

The lines are now too starkly drawn between the hard-line free traders, ideologues who brook no interference with the forces of the marketplace, and those with absolute faith in government intervention as the panacea. It is time for new policies that take advantage of the best in both; policies forward looking, flexible and tailored to the issue and the time.[1]

Martin and Susan Tolchin (1985)

There is a crying need for a new paradigm, *a* new understanding *of economic development and trade that is* consistent with the imperative of our time.[2]

Ravi Batra (1993)

The Logic of Warm-Bloodedness

The evolution of warm-bloodedness came as a logical step after exhausting all reptilian possibilities. The first reptilian possibility was cold-bloodedness which defined the option of no control on blood temperature and energy levels. Then came hibernation which prescribed the maximum dose of rigid control. Animals that applied a mix of cold-bloodedness and hibernation experimented with different doses of control in order to find the most successful amount. The next logical step was to explore what biologists call warm-blooded systems.

Designs of warm-blooded biological systems applied a new revolutionary way of control called feedback. The feedback control is automatic, flexible and adaptive to all the possibilities in the external environment. This type of control is in contrast to rigid hibernation control. The main idea of feedback control is that it can automatically trigger either warming or cooling actions, depending on whether the blood temperature is lower or higher than the desired value. Also, the amount of control needed to warm up or cool down the body is proportional to the difference between actual and desired blood temperatures.

If the actual blood temperature is below the desired one, the biological thermostat will reduce the flow of blood to the skin to decrease heat loss to the surroundings. If this is not enough to reach the desired blood temperature, the biological thermostat increases metabolism. In cases of extreme cold, the thermostat triggers shivering, which is a sort of involuntary physical activity to generate more internal heat. On the other hand, if the blood temperature is higher than the desired value, the biological thermostat triggers cooling actions such as expanding blood vessels at the skin to provide more heat exchange and also sweating and panting.

The logic of warm-bloodedness in trade should be similar to that in animals. We have exhausted all reptilian choices and found nothing that suits us as humans. The next logical step is to explore flexible, adaptive and advanced ways of government control on trade in what will be called warm-blooded trade systems. In order to have these systems as successful as warm-blooded biological systems, the trade systems must apply the same control type. This means that government control in trade policies must be automatic, flexible, adaptive and apply the concept of feedback.

In order to achieve this, the discretionary power of government officials (including the President and members of Congress) in setting trade polices should be entirely eliminated. Relying on government bureaucrats who play the dirty game of politics is as disappointing as having reptiles relying on discretion options to stabilize their blood temperature. The discretionary power of the government as well as the GATT and NAFTA treaties will be replaced by trade thermostats. These thermostats will be similar in theory and practice to biological thermostats of warm-blooded animals and also home heating and air-conditioning thermostats.

What Needs to Be Controlled in Warm-Bloodedness?

The first and most important step for any thermostat is to define what needs to be controlled and stabilized at desired levels and what that level should be. In warm-blooded animals, the answer is easy; blood temperature (or core body temperature) needs to be controlled, and the temperature should be stabilized around 98-99 degrees for most warm-blooded animals.

We need to apply the same logic in designing warm-blooded trade systems. This means that we need to define what should be controlled and stabilized at a desired level in trade thermostats, and what that level should be. Because we are facing a problem no one has tried to solve, we must expect controversies and different interpretations. I will describe my proposal for achieving warm-bloodedness in trade. I have to point out, though, that my proposal is just one of many possibilities.

Trade is equivalent to the blood in animals. Blood carries oxygen and needed nutrients to all different parts of the body. Trade carries all the needed raw materials and finished goods from all over the world to nourish domestic economies and satisfy the needs of consumers.

Trade balance represents the net effect of the trade flow for a particular nation and has the same importance as blood temperature. Trade balance determines how a nation consumes relative to how it produces. A surplus means that the nation exports more than it imports, or in other words, it produces more than it consumes. The difference between export and import results in accumulating more credit for the nation. On the other hand, a trade deficit means that the nation consumes more than it produces. The situation is like a person who spends more than he earns. In order to do so, the person has to borrow money. Likewise, debtor nations borrow from the rest of the world in order to finance their trade deficits. In both cases of individuals and nations, borrowing cannot continue forever.

Most countries hate large trade deficits as much as most animals dislike low levels of blood temperature. Nations suffering from large and persistent trade deficits are as vulnerable as animals suffering from persistently cold blood temperature. Cold-blooded animals lack the ability to produce the heat they need to maintain warm blood temperature. Likewise, debtor nations lack the ability to produce the goods they consume to maintain a healthy balance of trade. Respectable warm-blooded animals like mammals and birds never let their blood temperature drop or their activities become sluggish. Only primitive reptilian species do so. Respectable nations should treat themselves no less than warm-blooded animals, which means they should seek a warm level of trade balance. There should not be any excuse not to do so.

Now that we've identified trade balance as the equivalent to blood temperature in animals, the next logical question is what level of trade balance should warm-blooded nations seek? Should they seek surplus or zero balance? Most nations would like to have a surplus. However, this is impossible to achieve for all nations at the same time. In order for a few lucky nations to enjoy surplus, other unfortunate nations must suffer from deficit. If trade surplus is to be the definition of warm-bloodedness that would mean excluding many nations from warm-bloodedness, which is not acceptable.

In addition to excluding nations, having trade surplus as the goal creates another side effect. In order for nations to have a favorable trade balance, they need to increase trade restrictions. But they fail to see the vicious cycle that is generated. Here's how it works: flow of trade is as important as flow of blood in animals. Restricting such flow is uncomfortable for other trading nations. They will not stand still seeing the flow of their exports restricted and their export industries hurt. They are likely to retaliate by erecting more restrictions to the flow of imports. Once nations are caught in a wave of tit-for-tat, a trade war may start as happened during the aftermath of the Smoot-Hawley Hibernation Act of 1930. So targeting trade surplus cannot be the goal of warm-bloodedness in trade.

If we exclude both surplus and deficit from the desired level of trade balance in warm-blooded trade systems, the only choice left is zero balance. This is something all nations interested in warm-blooded trade can achieve at the same time. It is simple and fair. There would be no need to get into the never-ending argument of how high trade surplus should be. No nation would have any reason to complain or retaliate with a hostile restriction of imports. There would be no threat of trade wars. There would be no debtor or creditor nations. The world of trade would enjoy peace and harmony.

The next logical question is whether we should seek bilateral or multilateral trade balance. Bilateral balance means trade must be balanced between the U.S. and every single nation. Multilateral balance means that only the net trade between the U.S. and all other nations lumped together needs to be balanced. Under this definition, deficits and surpluses between the U.S. and any nation would be allowed as long as the net sum of trade is balanced.

The amount of control and trade restrictions needed for bilateral balance of trade is more than that needed for multilateral balance. This would result in a sharp reduction of volume and benefits of trade. Volume of trade is as important as volume of blood flow in animals. A healthy biological system needs more than just a stabilized, warm blood temperature. It also needs minimum restrictions to the flow of blood so that more oxygen and absorbed food can reach all parts of the body and support higher levels of activity. Similarly, a healthy warm-blooded trade system means more than just balancing trade. It means minimum trade restrictions and maximum volume of trade to support high levels of consumption of goods from all over the world. It is something only multilateral balance of trade can achieve.

Copying Warm-Bloodedness from Animals to Trade

Now we have identified multilateral trade balance as the goal, the next logical step is how to design a trade thermostat to achieve this goal for all nations interested in warm-blooded trade policy whether they are developing or developed. The trade thermostat must use the least amount of control in order to minimize restrictions and maximize the volume of trade. In addition, the success of the trade thermostats must be independent of what other nations are doing. In other words, it has to work properly in all conditions, irrespective of success in trade negotiations.

The most effective way to design a warm-blooded trade thermostat is to examine the biological thermostats of warm-blooded animals and copy their designs. One must be aware, however, that applying the biological ideas will not be just exact copying because of the differences between biological and trade systems. We need, therefore, to make some modifications and adjustments.

Overriding Discretionary Decisions

In warm-blooded animals, the decisions of the biological thermostat overrides the will of the animal. The blood temperature is stabilized regardless of what the animal is doing.

Similarly, in warm-blooded trade systems, the decisions of the trade thermostats must override the discretionary power of all government officials and all obligations to GATT and NAFTA. Trade must be stabilized irrespective of the personal views of the President and Congress and irrespective of the GATT and NAFTA treaties.

Triggering Opposite Actions

Biological thermostats have the ability to automatically trigger opposite actions as needed. These actions may be either to warm up or cool down the body.

Warm-blooded trade systems, too, must have the capability to automatically trigger opposite actions to slow down imports or to speed them up as needed in order to achieve balance of trade. This will be in contrast to the current situation in which government officials assume the responsibility of making discretionary decisions.

Logic of Corrective Actions

In warm-blooded animals, if the blood temperature is lower than the desired value, the corrective action is to conserve heat loss by restricting blood flow at the skin and peripherals. If the blood temperature is higher, the corrective action is to allow more heat disposal to surroundings by opening up blood vessels at the skin and peripherals.

Trade thermostats should apply the same principle. If the trade balance is deficit, the corrective action of the trade thermo-stat is to restrict the flow of imports. If the trade balance is surplus, the corrective action is to open up the flow of imports.

Corrective Actions and Needed Amount of Control

In biological thermostats, the signal to warm up or cool down the body is proportional to the difference between actual blood temperature and desired value. The higher the difference, the more correction is required.

Likewise, the correction signal produced by trade thermostats must be proportional to the amount of trade deficit or surplus. The higher the trade deficits, the higher will be the amount of corrected action to slow down imports. The higher the trade surplus, the higher will be the corrective action to open imports.

Implementing Corrective Actions in Trade

The next logical step is to define what is needed to be done in trade that represents the same effect as restricting or opening up blood vessels at the skin of warm-blooded animals. There are different ways to restrict or open up the flow of imports. These include increasing or relaxing trade control means such as tariffs, quotas and other import restrictions. Of all methods of trade control, tariffs are the simplest and easiest to implement. They generate revenue for governments which may be used to lower other taxes. All other methods of trade control are more complex and more rigid. They do not generate significant revenue for the government, and some of them even require more spending. They are more suited for trade hibernation than trade warm-bloodedness. This means in warm-blooded trade systems, only revenue tariffs will be allowed; all other means of trade control will be entirely eliminated.

We need to resolve one more issue before applying warm-bloodedness to trade. In warm-blooded animals, the biological thermostats control the blood temperature. The temperature is a good and broad indicator because it needs to be more or less the same whether the animal is large or small. We need to define something similar in trade systems that can be applied irrespective of the size of the economy. Trade deficit figures can give a distorted measurement for the status of trade. A trade deficit of one billion dollars is insignificant for the size of U.S. trade. It may be alarming, however, for a country with a small economy. We need to play a little mathematical trick to resolve this problem. Using the ratio of net trade deficit to total imports would be more meaningful than simply using trade deficit figures. It can be used effectively to guide trade thermostats to trigger the right amount of control to a broad range of nations regardless of the size of their economies or their trades. This would help in marketing trade thermostats to all nations interested in warm-blooded trade.

Now we have identified the indicator of trade control (or what control engineers call *error signal*) as the ratio of net trade balance to total imports and the method of control as revenue tariffs. Applying automatic feedback control means the corrective action must be proportional to the error signal. This means that in the case of deficits the control system would require increasing total tariffs per year by an amount, say 10 percent (or any other suitable value), of the ratio of net trade deficits to total imports. In the case of trade surplus it would require decreasing the total tariffs by the same ratio.

Distributing Corrective Actions among Trading Partners

The next step is to come up with a logic to distribute the increase or decrease of tariffs among nations with whom we trade. We cannot distribute the needed change in tariffs equally among all trading nations because they may have different practices in terms of opening or restricting their markets to our exports. The situation is comparable to what management of a typical company should do to distribute total salary increase or cuts to workers if the company earns or loses money. Distributing salary adjustments equally is not a good practice. It does not reward workers who excel or discourage lazy ones. Similarly, equal distribution of tariffs adjustment would not be a good practice. It does not reward nations that open up their doors to our exports or discourage protectionist nations that erect trade barriers.

Before companies makes salary adjustments they have to rank their workers. The trade thermostat should do the same thing, but in an automated and computerized way. This requires that government officials should keep their hands off such ranking. A simple, objective and automated ranking method would be to use the ratio of trade balance to imports for each nation as the ranking score. If the trade balance between the U.S. and a certain nation is a surplus, such nation would have positive ranking and would receive tariff reduction. If the trade balance is a deficit, then the nation would have negative ranking and would see their exports to the U.S. facing tariff increases. Such an automated ranking procedure for calculating tariff adjustment would assure fair, consistent and equal practice for all trading nations. Once the ranking figures are calculated, distributing total tariff increase or reduction among trading partners would be straightforward mathematical calculation that could be fully computerized.

With the suggested trade thermostat logic, the maximum tariff adjustment per year would be small, in the order of a few percentage points. This would give ample time to other nations to take voluntary actions to reduce trade deficits by opening their markets. If they do not take this action, the trade thermostat would gradually restrict their exports until the net trade is balanced. It would be more advantageous to those nations to open up their markets than to wait until the trade thermostat restricts their exports. They would have no reason to complain as the thermostat would apply the same rules equally to all nations.

One of the unique features of trade thermostats is that the external environment they deal with is what other nations are doing. Unlike the external environment of animals, the trade environment has intelligence. Other nations will eventually understand what trade thermostats can do and will voluntarily come up with their own actions before the thermostat does. Eventually the mere presence of trade thermostats will be enough to force nations to behave, open their markets and stop trying to exploit each other!

In brief, the trade thermostat replaces government discretion and GATT and NAFTA treaties with an automated and consistent decision-making device that is similar in design to biological thermostats of warm-blooded animals. Decision-making will be based on automatic feedback control logic using trade statistics. No longer will elected government officials use discretionary power to make decisions for the people that may be different than those promised in election campaigns. No longer will trade negotiators have the power to force their agreements on ordinary people and on the future of our children. With trade thermostats, intelligent market signals based on trade statistics will drive the decisions, using consistent logic.

Installing Warm-Bloodedness

Warm-blooded animals have a biological thermostat called the hypothalamus installed in their brains. Warm-blooded nations, too, should have something similar—economic thermostats installed in the brains of their economic and political systems. These may include business cycle thermostats, trade thermostats and any other needed thermostats.

Installing thermostats in our economic and political systems is different from those found naturally in animals. The people of each nation will have the power to create them. People will be the gods of their economic and trade systems; they will choose the thermostats that fit their needs the most. This means that when people cast their votes, they will elect economic thermostats as well as the president and Congress. In fact, electing economic thermostats will be more important and attract more attention in campaigns than electing government officials simply because the thermostats will have more power than elected officials.

Economic thermostats will be computer software that automates decision-making for stabilizing business cycles and balancing trade. They will apply feedback control concept like biological thermostats of warm-blooded animals, but using market statistics to drive the decision-making process. With the latest advances in computer technology, there should be no limit to the intelligence and sophistication of economic thermostats. There should be no reason why economic thermostats cannot achieve success similar to biological thermostats of warm-blooded animals. The intelligence of trade thermostats will be far superior to the current intelligence of government bureaucrats and trade negotiators.

Economic thermostats will be developed by private firms interested in profits as well as serving the people. Ideally, firms that develop economic and trade thermostats should hire biologists, engineers, economists and computer programmers. Biologists know exactly what warm-bloodedness can do for animals and what it should do for economic and trade systems. Engineers have a lot of practical expertise in applying automatic feedback control and should be able to master applying it in economic thermostats, too. Economists will communicate with biologists and engineers to translate what needs to be controlled. Programmers will transfer the suggestions of biologists, engineers and economists into the final computer code of the economic thermostat.

Designing and packaging economic thermostats should be treated the same as designing and packaging physical thermostats or any other products. They should be protected by patent rights. During the patent protection period, other competing thermostats would not be permitted to copy the logic of a certain thermostat without the permission of its firm. Such a practice that rewards innovators and inventors will create a new environment in economics and politics. In this environment, creative ideas will have a better opportunity to succeed than in the current situation that functions only by fooling people with political speeches and election campaign promises that have little to do with the reality.

Revisions to the economic thermostats will be allowed only at the beginning of the presidential election year (or mid-term election if we so choose). Between the time a new version is released and election day, people will have the opportunity to evaluate and compare different competing thermostats in a simulation mode. Once a thermostat is elected, its logic cannot be altered until the time of the new release at the next election.

The elected thermostat will not be the only one to receive full attention. People will have the opportunity to compare the decisions of the winning thermostat with other competing thermostats that did not win in the election. Summaries of the thermostats' decisions for the last several years will be presented in tables and graphs that are easy to understand. People will know which thermostat most often triggered the action needed the most. Once all the facts are objectively presented, choosing the right economic thermostat will be no harder than choosing the right home heating and air-conditioning thermostat!

As with business cycle thermostats, competition between trade thermostats will not be limited to American-made products. People may choose thermostats developed by foreign firms as well. American voters may elect Canadian, British, French, Japanese, German or Italian thermostats. Similarly, American thermostats will also compete in foreign markets. The larger global market will allow firms to justify more investment on developing and improving the economic thermostats, and thus improve their quality. More global competition means delivering better deals to people all over the world to serve their economic and trade needs. This will bring nations closer than ever before.

In brief, installing economic thermostats means dividing economic policies into several tasks such as stabilizing business cycles and balancing trade. The elected government politicians will have to give up their discretionary power. Competing firms from the private sector will take the responsibility of developing and marketing the thermostats. The thermostats will apply automatic feedback control similar to biological thermostats of warm-blooded mammals and birds. Like all computer software, the thermostats will be continuously evolving. People will have the power to decide which thermostat to be installed in their economic and political system. Even if people do not make the right installation choice during an election, they will have an opportunity to correct their mistakes and install a better thermostat at the next election.

The Warm-Blooded Reforms

Installing business cycle and trade thermostats in the brains of our political and economic systems will require revolutionary changes to the structure of our government. The election process will be different and will include electing economic thermostats in addition to government officials. These developments will require new *warm-blooded reforms* to change our constitution and branches and duties of the federal government.

In order to pass these reforms, we will need all the support we can get from the President, House and Senate. Currently, President Clinton and most members of Congress are committed to reptilism and are not likely to support the warm-blooded reforms. Any future elected government officials, whether Republican or Democrat, will probably be no different. Both the Republican and Democratic parties have had a long history supporting reptilian doctrines, whether cold-blooded conservative or hibernating liberal. They cannot change themselves. Their counterparts, the reptilian species, could not make any changes worthy of mention during the last 150 million years. Why should the reptilian species in the Republican and Democratic parties be any different?

Now that we have lost hope in the current reptilian parties, we need a new political party to adopt the warm-blooded reforms and rank them as number one issue on its agenda. The new party will be a new version of the current Reform Party called the *Warm-Blooded Reform Party*.

The new warm-blooded version will feature the newly evolved species of Warm-Blooded Reformist politicians. They will be the exact opposite of the current reptilian politicians who take pleasure in government power and making decisions that determine the fate of the people and their economic and trade systems, even if it means hurting the people and their future. The new politicians will give up the power to make discretionary decisions. They will acknowledge that they will yield to the decisions of the thermostats. They will settle for reduced duties, in return for ensuring that the thermostats' decisions are properly implemented. They will be happier knowing that they serve the people better that way.

Once one warm-blooded party in just one nation succeeds in implementing warm-blooded reforms to the constitution of its government, the entire world will have an opportunity to witness what warm-bloodedness can do to stabilize business cycles and balance and open trade. Then more and more nations will be willing to experiment with warm-bloodedness and give up reptilism.

By *dumping cold-blooded free trade and hibernating protectionism,* and by *installing warm-blooded reforms,* humans will follow exactly the same path that some fortunate, intelligent and advanced animals called mammals and birds followed when they *abandoned reptilism* and *sought warm-bloodedness!*

PART THREE

THE MISSING LINK BETWEEN HUMAN AND REPTILIAN SPECIES

10
The Reptilian Dynasty

Just because we think we're so wonderful doesn't mean we really are. We could be really terrible animals and never admit it because it would hurt so much.

Kurt Vonnegut (1990)

Extension of Class Reptilia in Economics and Politics

When biologists discover new animal species, they go back to their original classification of species and update it to reflect the recently discovered ones. In the first nine chapters of this book we have discovered many reptilian species dwelling in the habitats of economics and politics. We must do what biologists do. We must go back to the classification of *class reptilia* and *update* it to reflect the newly discovered economic and political species.

Chart 1 illustrates the proposed update for classification in class reptilia. As shown in this chart, class reptilia is divided into two main groups: *reptilian animals* and *reptilian humans*. Reptilian animals clearly belong to class reptilia; nobody would argue about it.

Chart 1
Universal Classification of Class Reptilia

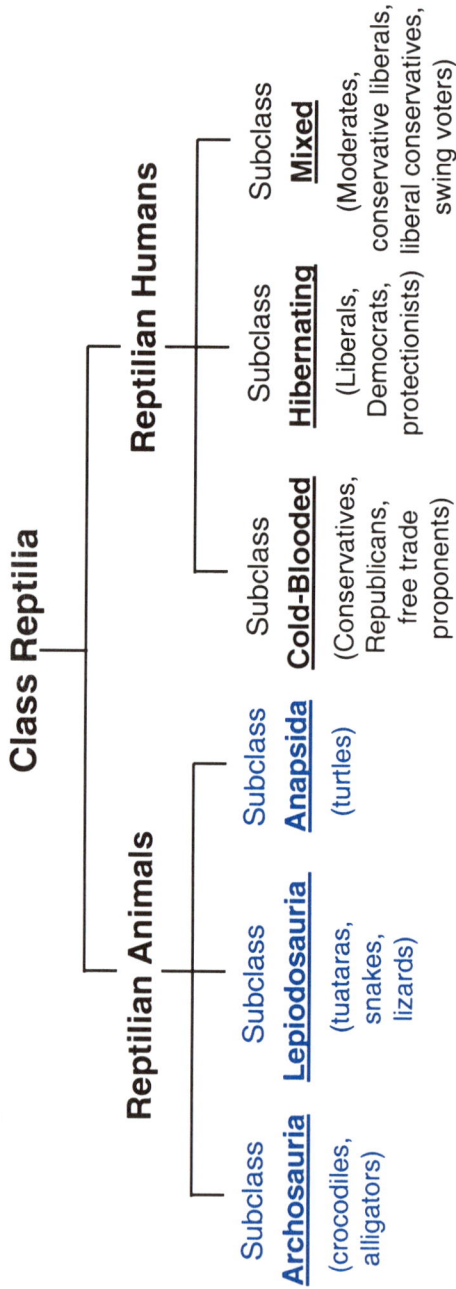

Class Reptilia

Reptilian Animals

Subclass
Archosauria
(crocodiles, alligators)

Subclass
Lepiodosauria
(tuataras, snakes, lizards)

Subclass
Anapsida
(turtles)

Reptilian Humans

Subclass
Cold-Blooded
(Conservatives, Republicans, free trade proponents)

Subclass
Hibernating
(Liberals, Democrats, protectionists)

Subclass
Mixed
(Moderates, conservative liberals, liberal conservatives, swing voters)

In contrast, reptilian humans do not have such a clear identity. They are weird. They belong biologically to *Homo sapiens*, the supreme species in the mammal class. Yet, they belong mentally to class reptilia in their economic, trade and political systems. Thus reptilian humans have a double identity: mammalian and reptilian. To understand the reptilian identity of humans we need to relate their classification to that of animals within class reptilia.

Classification of Reptilian Humans

Biologists have done a good job in classifying and organizing reptilian animals. This task is similar to organizing large companies into departments, plants, divisions and units. Likewise, biologists classify each animal class into orders, families, genus and species. We need to follow the footsteps of biologists and classify and organize the reptilian humans in a way that is *consistent* with the classification of reptilian animals.

Biologists divide reptilian animals into *three* basic groups called *subclasses*. The first group is subclass *archosauria* which includes 21 species of crocodiles and alligators. The second group is subclass *lepiodosauria* and includes about 5,700 species of lizards, snakes and tuatara (a New Zealand species). The third group is subclass *anapsida* with about 250 turtle species.

Reptilian humans, too, should have similar classifications. Reptilian humans comprise three main subclasses. Each subclass corresponds to and resembles its counterpart in reptilian animals. The first is *subclass cold-blooded* and includes conservatives and free trade proponents. Like their counterparts the crocodiles and alligators, the species of subclass cold-blooded are ferocious, savage and cold-blooded. The second group is *subclass hibernating* and comprises liberals, socialists, communists and protectionists. This subclass has a broad variety of different species varied in colors and shapes, which is similar to their reptilian counterpart, the subclass lepidosauria that features many snake and lizard species. The third group of reptilian humans is *subclass mixed* and includes the moderates, conservative liberals, liberal conservatives and swing voters. These species are too slow to be noticed in politics and economics, like their counterpart the turtles that move very slowly.

As shown in Chart 1, the *Independents* and *Reformists* are not officially a part of class reptilia anymore. During the Presidential election year 1992, they declared their *independence* from the reptilian dynasty and separated themselves from the reptilian Republicans and Democrats. Later, they sought *reforms* to evolve and become the mammal-like reptiles of our political system, leaving the true reptiles behind!

Orders of Reptilian Humans

Biologists divide each of the three surviving subclasses in the reptilian dynasty into smaller groups called *orders*. Likewise, we need to divide each of the three subclasses of reptilian humans into *orders*.

An effective way to divide reptilian humans into orders is to monitor the way they respond as they discover that they belong mentally to class reptilia. How do they feel about it? Then we can classify them according to the way they act. At present, reptilian humans are not aware that they belong mentally to class reptilia in their economic, trade and political systems. This book is the first to send a *wake-up* call to have them open their eyes to the reality in which they live and to seek new warm-blooded alternatives.

The wake-up call of this book is a message accusing all reptilian humans of betraying the mammal class and embracing the reptile class. As in any legal trial, the accused species may plead that they do or do not belong to class reptilia. The plea, whether guilty or not guilty, is an important key in under-standing the mentality of the suspect reptilian species and the way they should be classified.

As shown in Chart 2, there are four possible ways in which reptilian humans may respond: 1) admit belonging to class reptilia and be ashamed of it; 2) admit such belonging and be proud of it; 3) deny any connection with class reptilia; and 4) argue about such connection without clear admittance or clear denial. In other words, each of the four subclasses in class reptilia,

Chart 2

Classification of Reptilian Human Subclasses into Orders

Reptilian Human Subclasses

(subclass Cold-Blooded, Hibernating or Mixed)

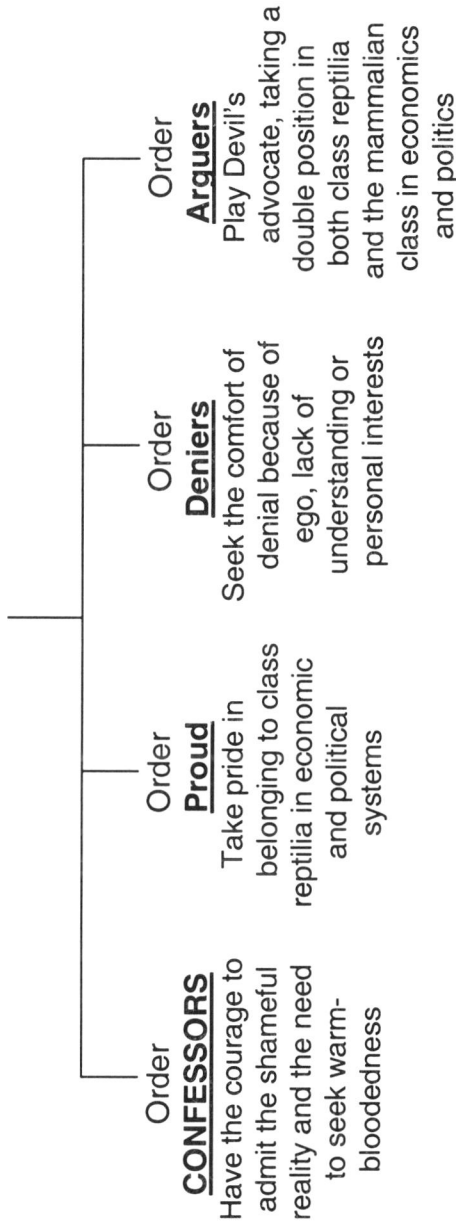

Order
CONFESSORS
Have the courage to admit the shameful reality and the need to seek warm-bloodedness

Order
Proud
Take pride in belonging to class reptilia in economic and political systems

Order
Deniers
Seek the comfort of denial because of ego, lack of understanding or personal interests

Order
Arguers
Play Devil's advocate, taking a double position in both class reptilia and the mammalian class in economics and politics

may be divided into four orders: *order confessors, order proud, order deniers* and *order arguers.*

The Courage to Confess the Shameful Reality

The great majority of people will be shocked to hear the claims that all current economic, trade and political species belong to class reptilia. After they recover from the first shock, some people will show signs of understanding the ideas and evidence presented in this book. Then, they will confess that they belong mentally to class reptilia. Some Republicans will admit that they are cold-blooded reptilian species. By the same token, some Democrats will acknowledge that they are true hibernators. Whether cold-blooded, hibernators or mixed they will be ashamed of their position in class reptilia. After all, they biologically belong to the most superior warm-blooded mammalian species, which deserves nothing less in economics and politics.

As those individuals open their eyes to the sad reality and the way they have been deceived by economists, politicians and the media they will boil with anger. These individuals have been hearing nothing but simplistic reptilian views, either cold-blooded conservative or hibernating liberal, repeated over and over again.

The boiling outrage of those individuals and the agony, humiliation and shame they suffer will serve a good purpose. It will give them the will to change, escape from class reptilia and flee into the warm-blooded class. This situation is like trying to escape from Earth's gravitational field and flee into outer space. You would need a powerful rocket to do so. Similarly to break all the remaining ties with the reptilian dynasty in economics and politics, one needs a huge emotional thrust ignited by shock and fueled by humiliation, outrage and shame.

Proud to Be Reptilian

In contrast to the first group that will be ashamed to belong to class reptilia, there will be another group who will feel proud of such a relationship! Like the first group, the proud group will also acknowledge the analogy between biological systems and economic and political systems. They will admit that it is possible to apply warm-bloodedness in economics and politics the same way it has been applied in biological systems. They will not agree, however, about the argument that true warm-blooded mammals and birds are superior to cold-blooded and hibernating reptiles. By the same token, they will deny that warm-blooded economic, trade and political systems would be superior to reptilian systems.

Surprisingly, the proponents of this group will argue that reptiles are indeed superior to warm-blooded mammals and birds. Their argument takes the following scenario. Most reptiles became extinct at the late Cretaceous Period because of a mysterious incidence, possibly an asteroid crash. Without such an incident, the majority of reptiles would had survived and evolved into species that would rule the planet, including all the mammal and bird species. Planet Earth would have been a better place if we humans have evolved from reptilian rather than warm-blooded mammalian origin. The sad reality is that we can't change the past. However, we can control the present and the future. While the hope for reptilian superiority in biological species is gone forever, there is still hope in preserving the superiority of reptilian economic and political species for a long time.

With such a philosophical but deceptive argument, this group is likely to be the most bizarre group in the reptilian dynasty. After all, being proud to belong to class reptilia is as weird as being proud to worship Satan and evil.

The Comfort of Denial

The third group in each subclass of the reptilian dynasty is the group of deniers. Unlike the earlier two groups who admit that they belong to class reptilia, the people of this group will deny the existence of reptilian species in economic, trade and political systems. They will argue that the analogy between biological systems and economic/political systems does not make sense to them. The existing economic systems are not as awful as claimed here. The warm-blooded systems wouldn't be much better than the existing ones. The idea of classifying economic and political systems according to cold-bloodedness, hibernation and warm-bloodedness will add nothing but confusion.

Like most cases of denying sad reality, there are three major causes of denial: 1) ego problem, 2) lack of ability to understand, and 3) personal benefits from the existing reality.

People with big egos will be hesitant to admit that they have been fooled. That is particularly true for many reptilian humans. It will be hard for them to admit that they have been fooled by current politicians, economists and the media into the reptilian situation in which we have been trapped. It is not easy to admit that with all the advances of science, technology and computers, our economic, trade and political systems are reptilian and more primitive than the warm-blooded biological systems of mice, rats, pigs and turkeys.

In addition to an ego problem, some people will deny the proposed similarity between economic/political systems and biological systems because they lack understanding of the simple basics in science and biology. While they still can understand science basics if they spend some time doing so, it is easier for them to do nothing and deny the existence of any problem in the first place. Thus they choose to be lazy and accept the reptilian reality in economics and politics rather than spending time and effort educating themselves in science so that they can understand the similarity between biological systems and economic and political systems.

The third and last category of the deniers are those who have personal or financial interests in preserving the current reptilian system. They may be people who have spent many years as prestigious economists and politicians. They may see the rise of warm-blooded economic and political systems as a threat to their image, careers or income.

In approaching any person from the groups of the deniers, an effective strategy is to narrow down the main motivation behind his or her denial, whether it is ego, lack of understanding of science, or personal and financial interests. Once you know the weakest point of the denier, you can concentrate on hammering this point relentlessly until the person comes to his or her senses and admits belonging to class reptilia!

Playing Devil's Advocate

The fourth and last group in each subclass of the reptilian dynasty is the group of arguers. Unlike the earlier three groups that either clearly admit or deny belonging to class reptilia, this group takes a vague position. People from this group will argue that the analogy between biological systems and economic and political systems seem to be interesting, innovative and plausible but not necessarily true or practical. They will indicate that they need to see more evidence to support the classification of economic and political systems according to cold-bloodedness, hibernation and warm-bloodedness. They will consider confessing that they belong to class reptilia in economic and political beliefs once they see more convincing arguments, more academic work and the results of testing actual warm-blooded economic, trade and political systems.

The people of this reptilian group are reluctant and not sure. They do not want to make a clear commitment either 100 percent for class reptilia or 100 percent for the warm-blooded mammalian class in economics and politics. Like many cases in life, reluctant people are too slow to grip wonderful opportunities, especially if such opportunities require too much change and taking the risk of trying the unknown.

Running away from class reptilia to the mammal class is *a wonderful opportunity* offered only to the last generation of the *Dark Age of Reptilian Economics and Politics*, during the beginning of the new millennium. This opportunity, however, requires major changes. It requires abandoning the reptilian parties, whether Republican or Democrat, and joining the new Warm-Blooded Reform Party. It also requires abandoning economic sciences and typical economists who practice it and seeking a new discipline of bio-economic engineering and new professionals of bio-economic engineers. The new opportunity requires closing the eyes and ears to all media channels that fool people with reptilian views in economics and politics.

These fundamental changes are too drastic, too revolutionary and too daring. Not many people have the courage and the will to make such changes that would frighten ordinary persons. Only extraordinary and tough individuals can cope with these unusual changes.

Despite the anxiety and risks associated with such changes, warm-blooded economic and political systems offer new promises and big dreams. The rewards of economic and political warm-bloodedness are tempting, even if just a small fraction of the promised claims could be achieved.

Thus hesitant people face a serious dilemma. There are risks in making major changes, too early, to evolve from reptilian to warm-blooded mammalian species in economics and politics. At the same time there are huge, tempting rewards. In order to avoid the risk and at the same time not to miss the reward, some individuals will be tempted to play the trick of devil's advocate. In this strategy, you need not take a clear position opposing or supporting warm-blooded economics and politics. You just sit back, argue and demand more intellectual evidence and more test results until you become totally convinced of the need to abandon the reptilian dynasty.

The devil's advocates will try to position themselves strategically between the reptilian dynasty and the mammalian dynasty in economics and politics. If the warm-blooded mammalian movement fails, they would lose nothing by playing devil's advocate. Even in such a case, they should be considered more open and more supportive of new ideas than the group of deniers. If the warm-blooded movement wins, they can claim that they showed some support and some sympathy during its early stages. They can add that by playing devil's advocate, they gave the warm-blooded thinkers more incentives and pushed them to develop even better answers.

Playing devil's advocate within the reptilian dynasty may seem, at first glance, like a clever strategy to position oneself without taking any risks or missing rewards. Those who are tempted to consider such a strategy should be reminded that the best positions in the warm-blooded mammalian dynasty in economics and politics will be filled early by swift species from the confessors group. If devil's advocates overdo it, they will have to settle for the remaining low ranks in the mammalian dynasty in economics and politics.

Future of the Reptilian Dynasty

Belonging to the reptilian dynasty in economics and politics is an insult to the intelligence of every human being. We humans deserve much better than that. We deserve a warm-blooded mammalian dynasty. To have the dream of the warm-blooded dynasty come true, we must destroy the human version of the reptilian dynasty.

A key step to accomplish this goal is to educate everyone about this evil dynasty, its connection with primitive reptiles and extinct dinosaurs, and its classification into subclasses, orders and species. Once intelligent citizens understand such classification and the similarity in features and destiny between reptilian humans and reptilian animals, they will become more educated and more capable of bringing an end to the reptilian dynasty.

The first sign of internal collapse within the reptilian dynasty will begin with many species of the order *confessors* admitting in an agony of shame and humiliation that they belong to such a dynasty. On the positive side, those species will be proud to desert the reptilian dynasty and join the warm-blooded dynasty.

Next to the species of confessors, more species from the arguers will follow. They will find satisfying answers to everything they have asked or argued about. They will receive more intellectual evidence to support the analogy between economic/political systems and biological systems. They will see the successful establishment and rise of warm-blooded parties all over the world. They will be impressed by the scientific approach of bio-economic engineering that will be a major milestone in bridging the natural and social sciences. With those developments, they will find it harder to play devil's advocate any longer. Finally, they will yield, admit their belonging to class reptilia and flee to the warm-blooded class.

The flight of the species of confessors and arguers from the reptilian dynasty will shock the remaining reptilian species. Many deniers will not be able to deny any longer. Many *knees* from these species *shall bow* to warm-blooded supremacy in economics and politics! And many *tongues shall confess* that the *Dark Age of Reptilian Economics and Politics* must end soon, and a

New *Bright Age of Warm-blooded Mammalian Economics and Politics* must begin!

With the loss of all sensible species in the human version of the reptilian dynasty, there will be nothing left but a few species that are *too slow, too stubborn and too rigid.* And such a *bizarre collection of fools* is what the reptilian dynasty in economics and politics deserves!

11
Warm-Bloodedness in the Eyes of Reptiles

Every man takes the *limits of his own field of vision* for the *limits of the world.*

Schopenhauer (1851)

You *only see* what *your eyes want to see.*

Madonna and Patrick Leonard (1998 song)

Being Objective or Subjective

If reptiles had magically changed and became intelligent creatures for a little while and could compare their species with those of warm-blooded mammals and birds, it would be interesting to know how they would perceive their position in the animal kingdom. Would they be objective, acknowledging their primitive reality and admitting that they are inferior to warm-blooded mammals and birds? Or would they be subjective and defensive, dominated by their ego and insisting that they are the best class in the animal kingdom?

Of course, these thoughts and questions will never go through the minds of reptilian animals. They are lucky not to have to confront their positions in the animal kingdom. Reptilian humans, however, will be different as they can't escape the confrontation: While reptilian humans belong to class reptilia in their economic, trade and political systems, they are the supreme species in the mammal class. In spite of the nonsense and inferiority in economic and political systems, they have intelligence, curiosity and the ability to reason in other areas. Even if they seem to accept reptilian systems, they can not prevent themselves from thinking about warm-blooded alternatives and how they are compared to reptilian ones.

Warm-Bloodedness in the Eyes of Cold-Blooded Species

If cold-blooded reptiles that never hibernate had the ability to think and compare themselves to warm-blooded animals, they would come up with bizarre arguments. True cold-blooded reptiles oppose all kinds of biological regulations of blood temperature and energy levels, whether hibernating or warm-blooded. They would argue that such regulatory systems interfere with an animal's free will and enjoyment and that animals are capable of regulating their blood temperature using free behavioral options, and therefore, do not need any regulatory system.

In the eyes of cold-blooded reptiles, all regulatory systems are more or less the same. They would not be able to differentiate between warm-bloodedness and hibernation. Cold-blooded reptiles would fail to recognize the importance of warm-bloodedness as the key in making mammals and birds the supreme vertebrate classes in the animal kingdom.

What will never in fact go on in the minds of cold-blooded reptiles in our imaginary scenario will take place in the minds of cold-blooded reptilian humans in the real world. You just need to translate the words of cold-blooded reptiles from biological to economic and political notations.

Cold-blooded reptilian humans include two main categories: conservatives and free trade proponents. Conservatives oppose all kinds of economic regulations to stabilize business cycles. They believe that such regulations interfere with economic and political freedoms, and that there is no need for regulations as free behavioral options of firms and individuals are adequate for achieving best economic results. Since conservatives have never seen any economic or trade thermostat before, their extremists would put warm-blooded systems in the same category as the hibernating systems of their liberal enemies.

Unlike this simplistic group, sophisticated conservatives will recognize that the type and intensity of control in economic thermostats are different from those in government regulations and discretion of politicians and the Federal Reserve Board. While most conservatives prefer no regulations at all—like their close relatives the cold-blooded reptiles—the sophisticated group would pick economic and trade thermostats rather than typical government regulations and discretion if they were forced to choose between these two alternatives.

Another conservative group will see the rise of warm-blooded regulatory systems as an opportunity to hurt their liberal enemies and even force them into extinction. With those warm-blooded systems, there will be no need for liberal hibernation if the economic climate becomes cold. And those warm-blooded systems are closer to conservative values of less government size and power.

But other conservative groups will predict the real danger from the rise of warm-blooded species. They will realize that once people try warm-blooded government and experiment with economic thermostats, they will never go back and vote for conservative politicians again. Because of such threat to the survival of the conservative movement and the Republican Party, some conservatives would prefer to lose to their liberal enemies rather than to the new warm-blooded species. Therefore, they will rank economic warm-bloodedness as number one enemy on their list, even before liberal hibernation.

These possible scenarios of what will go on in the minds of conservatives will happen also to free trade proponents. Like conservatives opposing government control on the economy, free trade proponents oppose all kinds of government control on imports. With this perception, strict free trade proponents will see trade thermostats as not much different than typical hibernation control of protectionism.

On the other hand, realistic free trade proponents will recognize that protectionism is more the rule than the exception in trade. If those hibernating nations could be convinced to change their trade policies from protectionism to warm-bloodedness, and if they were to remove all their trade barriers and replace them with trade thermostats, that would be in the interest of free trade. After all, trade thermostats would allow less control and less restriction than typical protectionism. Also, the spread of warm-blooded trade policy would prevent the reoccurrence of trade wars like the one that happened in the aftermath of the Smoot-Hawley Hibernation Act of 1930. Some free trade proponents, therefore, would love to see the nations that practice protectionism change to warm-blooded trade policies. Then, it would be much easier for the U.S. to continue practicing free trade.

Apart from this group, other free trade proponents will recognize the threat from the rise of warm-bloodedness in trade. They will predict that once a single nation tries trade thermostats, all other nations will see what warm-bloodedness can deliver. Warm-blooded policies will allow more volume of trade than typical free trade, will balance trade deficits, stabilize currency and provide fairness for all trading nations. With all these advantages, the real threat to the future of free trade will come from warm-blooded trade not from protectionism.

Warm-Bloodedness in the Eyes of Hibernating Species

Hibernating species would see the warm-blooded alternative as inadequate for survival. They would argue that in a cold, harsh environment there is no other alternative to preserve life but to give up all sense of living and accept the hibernation coma.

Again, this type of mentality will be found in the minds of hibernating humans: liberals and protectionists. Many liberals also will have a hard time accepting the idea of replacing the discretionary power of government bureaucrats and the Federal Reserve board with economic thermostats as this means reducing the size of federal government and the power of politicians in setting economic policies. Protectionists too would feel the same way about eliminating politicians' rule and power in trade negotiations and replacing them with trade thermostats.

In contrast to the negative feelings of those hibernating species that are skeptical about the importance and potential of warm-bloodedness, other species will see the rise of warm-bloodedness as an opportunity to defeat their enemies, the cold-blooded conservatives and free trade proponents. A third group will recognize that the real danger for the future of liberalism and protectionism will come from warm-bloodedness rather than from conservatism and free trade.

Warm-Bloodedness in the Eyes of Mixed Species

Species that alternate between cold-bloodedness and hibernation during the warm and cold seasons would have no strong argument against warm-bloodedness. They know from practical experience that it feels good to enjoy living and minimize hibernation as much as possible. On the other hand, it is crucial to preserve life in cold, harsh environments. Both living to full potential and preserving the survival of species are equally important. And both are maximized in the warm-blooded altern-ative.

What would go on in the mind of animal species that alternate between cold-bloodedness and hibernation will also go on in the mind of the humans who compromise between conservatism and liberalism such as moderates, liberal conservatives, conservative liberals, Independents and Reformists. These species know the danger of having governments that apply a hands-off approach during cold economic environments. They also know the problems associated with big governments that try to rigidly regulate all economic activities. These moderate species are fed up with conservative and liberal sermons that preach either too little or too much government. They know that these deceptive sermons never worked in the real world, and will never work.

These mixed species will be open the most to warm-blooded economic policies. While economic and trade thermostats will eliminate the power of politicians and bureaucrats in economic and trade policies, the government will not apply a hands-off approach to serious economic problems like typical conservative governments.

Mixed species will see warm-blooded economics and politics as an opportunity for forging a clear political identity that distinguishes them from other reptilian species. The new identity will be in the form of a new party dedicated to the moderate middle. After all, the Republican Party is dedicated to the cold-blooded right and the Democratic Party is dedicated to the hibernating left. The warm-blooded middle deserves a new, dedicated identity, not a vague mix of the right and left.

Seeing Limits on Field of Vision as the Limits of the World

While the mixed species led by the Independents and Reformists will be lucky to look objectively at warm-bloodedness and seek it, most reptilian species will not be able to see its full potential. The reason is not because of limits of warm-bloodedness but because of limitations in their own field of vision! *They can't see because they choose to see only what their eyes want to see!* As Madonna's song implies, *they are frozen* in class reptilia because of the way they see things!

Those species with limited and distorted vision may survive for a little while ruling the habitats of economics and politics. But the existence of impaired vision and inferior mentality at the top of the ruling pyramid is not a stable situation. It can't continue much longer. Sooner or later these species will collapse under the attack of the warm-blooded species that will have the advantages of sharp vision and superior intelligence. Only then, the reptilian species in the Republican and Democratic Parties will be *forced to see what they have refused to see,* namely the rise and supremacy of warm-bloodedness in economics and politics!

12
Choose Your Own Species

Guess if you *can*, *choose* if you *dare*.
Pierre Corneille (Heraclius, 1646)

Mankind are more disposed to *suffer*, while evils are sufferable, than to *right themselves by abolishing the forms to which they are accustomed*.
Thomas Jefferson
Declaration of Independence, July 4, 1776

No man *chooses evil* because it is evil; he only *mistakes it for happiness*, the good he seeks.
Mary Wollstonecraft
A Vindication of the Rights of Men (1790)

We are the *first* species to *have taken our evolution into our own hands*.
Carl Sagan (1979)

Check-up of Mental Health in Economics and Politics

Physicians recommend that their patients go for frequent physical examination, typically once a year. In such examinations, physicians check up on several things such as breathing, blood pressure and heart condition. They request blood samples and monitor medical problems that vary from patient to patient. Even people in excellent health are urged to go for physical check-ups.

People need another kind of check-up for possible mental health problems in their economic and political beliefs. Most people do not know yet that belonging to class reptilia in economic, trade and political systems is a serious *mental disease!* Indeed it is *insanity.* This insanity has two basic forms: cold-bloodedness and hibernation. All conservatives and free trade proponents suffer from the syndrome of cold-bloodedness. All liberals, socialists, communists and protectionists suffer from the syndrome of hibernation to varying degrees. Even moderates have problems too, although their symptoms are less serious. They suffer from a syndrome called mix and compromise between conservative cold-bloodedness and liberal hibernation.

Mental health professionals have not yet acknowledged these devastating syndromes as mental problems. Until they recognize that belonging to class reptilia is a serious mental illness, people are on their own.

Even if mental professionals recognize this mental illness, that wouldn't do much good either. In most physical and mental illnesses, patients sincerely want to be cured. In the mental illness of belonging to class reptilia, this is not the case. In fact, suffering from this illness is a free choice. People could cure themselves instantly any time they want. They are mentally sick because they choose to be mentally sick.

In addition to the attitude of mental patients in economics and politics, the attitude of professionals makes it even worse. Unlike the mental health field in which professionals try sincerely to cure their patients, most professional economists and politicians are infected by the same mental diseases and try to spread them to as many people as possible!

An interesting trend in economics and politics is how patients and professionals look at themselves and others. Although most people may have problems in recognizing that they are mentally sick as they belong to class reptilia, they correctly diagnose that their opponents are mentally sick. For instance, conservatives correctly diagnose that liberals are mentally sick because liberals suffer from symptoms of hibernation. Yet, conservatives believe that cold-bloodedness is not a mental problem. On the other hand, liberals correctly diagnose that conservatives are mentally sick because conservatives suffer from symptoms of cold-bloodedness. Yet, liberals believe that hibernation is not a mental problem.

The same story happens too in the habitats of trade. You just need to replace conservatives with free trade proponents and liberals with protectionists.

In order to settle the never-ending arguments about who is mentally sick and who is not, every person has to forget about the mental problems of others. Every human has to look at his or her own choice of which economic and political species to select. Unlike animals that do not have much choice over selecting their own species, *humans can take economic and political evolution into their own hands!* Humans have the choice to be either 1) *cold-blooded*, 2) *hibernating*, 3) *mix* of cold-blooded and hibernating, and 4) *warm-blooded*. People must have frequent check-ups of their mentality to reexamine their economic and political beliefs. In these check-ups they need to be objective and carefully investigate the symptoms, the advantages and disadvantages of belonging to each of these four choices so that they can cure themselves and help cure others.

Mental Health Check-up Must be at Least Annual

No matter how excellent your physical health is, you need to have an annual examination. The same is true about your mental health concerning your beliefs in economics and politics. No matter how superior you think your economic and political species is and how smart your choice compared to other dumb choices, you need to have a thorough annual examination. Then you can weigh all the facts and make a judgment call of whether to continue to be a member of your current species or jump into another one.

Recommended Timing for Annual Mental Check-up

Patients can go for an annual physical check-up any time if they don't have an immediate problem. Mental patients in economics and politics are different. There is a an ideal time for their annual mental check-up: either before the *New Year's Eve* or before the *election day*.

During New Year's Eve, people look back at the last year. They think about what they did, the things they liked and the things they didn't like. It may be a useful time for people to reexamine their economic and political species. They should evaluate what they liked and what they didn't like about cold-bloodedness, hibernation and mix of both in the year about to end. Then they can decide whether in the new year they should continue to be the same reptilian species, switch to another kind of reptilian species or evolve to warm-blooded species.

The coming of the new millennium (officially January 1, 2001) will be an excellent opportunity for such self-examination. This new millennium will arrive after more than two centuries that have witnessed the rise and dominance of reptilism in economics and politics. Individuals must think about what they want to be in the new millennium. Should they be reptilian like all species that rose in the last two centuries? Or should they be warm-blooded mammalian like the species that will rise in the new millennium?

In addition to a self-check before New Year's Eve, responsible citizens should have another one before each election. During this time, voters choose the kind of economic and political species they believe would fit the needs of our nation. Typically, conservatives want cold-blooded species to always rule in economics and politics. On the other hand, liberals prefer hibernating species. Moderates try to see whether conservative cold-bloodedness or liberal hibernation is more suitable for the current economic environment. Before voters cast their votes for which kind of species should rule our economic and political system, they should examine which kind of species they want themselves to be.

Not all elections receive equal attention. Presidential elections gets the lion's share. Mid-term elections (such as in 2002) receive less attention while years of odd numbers (like 2001) are stagnant.

So, voters should go through a self check-up for their mental health in economics and politics before mid-term elections and presidential elections. But the check-up should be more thorough during the presidential elections. The coming presidential election of the year 2000 will be even more special than any other presidential election in history as it will be the first in the new millennium.

Quick Service for Mental Check-up

The main purpose of this book is to inform readers about how to examine, evaluate and choose their own species. Since this examination should be done either once or twice a year, it wouldn't be practical to ask people to read this book again every time they reexamine their own species. That would take many hours. Therefore, there is a need to provide a *quick service* to let people *thoroughly* evaluate the choice of their species in *less than an hour*. This is almost as fast as "no-wait quick lube job" for your car.

If you would like to access such quick service and avoid the need to read many pages, turn the page to Table 1: *Factors You Should Consider to Choose Your Own Species*. This table provides a concise 6-page summary of what we have talked about in detail in the last eleven chapters, highlights the key items and features to help readers choose their species. Digesting this table shouldn't take more than an hour.

In order to make maximum use of Table 1, you should read through it twice. During the first time, just scan it quickly to get an overall picture of the process of self-examining your species. Don't take what is written in this table as absolute truth, but as just suggestions to stimulate your thinking as you search for answers. There will be things you will like in my suggestions and things you will hate. Let us be open-minded and tolerate difference in opinions. If you don't agree on a certain factor or item, feel free to cross it out and write your own personal comments instead. I wouldn't feel bad if you correct me.

You should be aware, however, that your personal views and corrections may vary from year to year as you go through the same self-exam. I recommend, therefore, that you make a copy of

Table 1 every time you go through the self-exam and leave the original table unmarked. I also recommend that you keep your notes and corrections for your personal record. Later, you or your children will be interested to look at these records to know how fast your species evolved over time from reptilian to mammalian form.

After quick overview of Table 1, you should go through it again at a slower and more thorough pace. During the second time you will write down the score for each of the four species and repeat that for all the 31 factors in Table 1. You may use Table 2 to organize and document these scores. In this Table, you may assign each factor an equal weight of 10 points. You need to think carefully for a couple of minutes about each factor and distribute the 10 points between the four types of species that include 1) cold-blooded, 2) hibernating, 3) mixed and 4) warm-blooded. If you like a certain species, give it the lion's share of the score. If you don't like it, give it a little share. If you hate it, simply give it a zero score. For instance, a typical conservative may give cold-blooded, hibernating, mixed and warm-blooded species a score of 8, 0, 0 and 2 points respectively. On the other hand, a typical liberal would give a score of 0, 8, 0 and 2 points respectively.

It is not easy to predict how most Independents and Reformists distribute their score as they are abused the most in politics. After all, they lack clear identity and fair recognition as they represent the mammal-like reptiles of our political system. It wouldn't be surprising if they give the warm-blooded species the entire 10 points as that may be their only hope to get out of the desperate situation of being overshadowed by the true reptiles—the conservatives and liberals.

Whether you are a cold-blooded conservative, hibernating liberal or desperate Independent/Reformist, write down the score for each of the four species in Table 2. Then add the individual scores and write the results at the bottom row marked "final score."

Table 1: Factors You Should Consider to Choose Your Own Species

Factor	Cold-Blooded Species	Hibernating Species	Mixed Species	Warm-Blooded Species
Biological Applications	Exclusively in reptile class (for terrestrial applications)	Mostly reptiles class (some applications of mix with warm-bloodedness persist in mammal and bird classes)	Mix between cold-bloodedness and hibernation is common in reptile class	Exclusively in mammal and bird classes
Economic/ Political Applications	Republicans	Democrats (deeper hibernation levels are found in socialists and communists)	Moderates, conservative liberals, liberal conservatives and swing voters	Warm-blooded Reformists
Trade Applications	Free Trade	Protectionism	Middle ground between free trade and protectionism	Warm-blooded trade policy
Biological Principles	No control on blood temperature. Relies entirely on free behavior options.	Rigid, excessive control during hibernation coma. Nothing is left for free behavioral options.	Less intense and shorter duration of hibernation control	Automatic feedback control. Enhancing free behavioral options and maximizing preserving life.
Economic/ Political Principles	No government control on economy. Relies mostly on free behavioral options of firms and individuals.	Rigid, excessive government control on economy. Little is left for free options.	Less intense and shorter duration of government control on economy.	Installing business cycle thermostats. Enhancing freedom and maximizing economic stability.
Trade Principles	No government control on trade. Relies entirely on free options of firms and individuals.	Rigid, excessive government control on trade. Little is left for free options.	Less amount and shorter duration of government control on trade.	Installing trade thermostats. Enhancing freedom and maximizing trade and currency stability.

Table 1 (Continued) : Factors You Should Consider to Choose Your Own Species

Factor	Cold-Blooded Species	Hibernating Species	Mixed Species	Warm-Blooded Species
Biological Advantages	Freedom from hibernation control; enhanced efficiency and more life enjoyment	Preserving life and species survival in cold environment	Combining advantages of cold-bloodedness and hibernation, but at less degree	Combining and exceeding advantages of cold-bloodedness and hibernation
Economic/ Political Advantages	Freedom from government control; enhanced economic efficiency and more enjoyment	Preserving financial survival of working and lower classes in cold economic conditions	Combining advantages of conservatism and liberalism, but at less degree	Combining and exceeding advantages of conservatism and liberalism
Trade Advantages	Freedom from government control; enhanced efficiency and enjoying foreign goods	Preserving industrial base and workers threatened by cold, global environment	Combining advantages of free trade and protectionism, but at less degrees	Combining and exceeding advantages of free trade and protectionism
Biological Disadvantages	Excessive swings in blood temperature; increased vulnerability in cold environment	Submission to rigid, excessive control. Loss of sense of living and freedom	Combining disadvantages of cold-bloodedness and hibernation, but at less degree	None
Economic/ Political Disadvantages	Excessive swings in business cycles; increased vulnerability in cold economic environment	Submission to rigid, excessive government control on economy. Sacrificing freedom.	Combining disadvantages of conservatism and liberalism, but at less degrees	None
Trade Disadvantages	Excessive swings in trade deficits and currency exchange rates; increased vulnerability from cold global competition	Submission to rigid, excessive government control on trade. Sacrificing freedom of consumers and firms.	Combining disadvantages of free trade and protectionism, but at less degrees	None

Table 1 (Continued) : Factors You Should Consider to Choose Your Own Species

Factor	Cold-Blooded Species	Hibernating Species	Mixed Species	Warm-Blooded Species
Biological Environmental Factor	Reptiles are attracted to cold-bloodedness during tropical climates	Animals seek hibernation during cold climates	Reptiles pursue mix of cold-bloodedness in hibernation during seasonal climates	Warm-bloodedness is well suited for all climates whether tropical, seasonal or cold
Economic/ Political Environmental Factors	People and nations are attracted to conservatism during favorable economic climates	People and nations seek liberalism and socialism during cold economic climates	Moderates multiply during periods of seasonal economic climates	Warm-blooded economic policy is well suited for all economic climates
Trade Environmental Factors	People and nations are attracted to free trade during favorable global climates	People and nations seek protectionism during freezing global climates	Mix between free trade and protectionism become convincing during periods of seasonal global climates	Warm-blooded trade policy is well suited for all global climates
Biological Body Size Factors	Reptiles of gigantic sizes (dinosaurs) are attracted the most to cold-bloodedness	Vulnerable animals of little size need hibernation	Average size reptiles generally apply mix of cold-bloodedness and hibernation	Warm-bloodedness is well suited to a wide range of body size
Economic/ Political Size Factors	Rich people and nations are attracted to conservatism	Vulnerable people and nations need liberalism and socialism	Middle class are attracted to mix between conservatism and liberalism	Warm-blooded economic policy is well suited to a wide range of rich and poor people and nations
Trade Size Factors	Rich nation and people are attracted to free trade	Vulnerable people and nations need protectionism	Middle class are attracted to mix between free trade and protectionism	Warm-blooded trade policy is well suited to a wide range of rich and poor people and nations

Table 1 (Continued) : Factors You Should Consider to Choose Your Own Species

Factor	Cold-Blooded Species	Hibernating Species	Mixed Species	Warm-Blooded Species
Biological Performance	Fairly good in tropical climates, fatal in cold climates and poor on average basis	Good in freezing climates, terrible in tropical climates and poor on overall basis	Nothing particularly good; poor on overall basis	Excellent in all conditions
Economic/ political Performance	Fairly good in favorable economic climates; fatal in freezing eras like the Great Depression; poor on overall level	Fairly good in cold economic climates such as the Great Depression, poor on overall level	Nothing particularly good in any economic period; poor on overall level	Excellent in all economic conditions
Trade Performance	Fairly good in favorable global climates; bad in freezing climates; poor on overall basis	Disappointing in all economic conditions, even during the Great Depression	Nothing particularly good in any period; poor on overall level	Excellent in all conditions of global climates
Characteristics of Species	Primitive, inferior and miserable whether in animals or economic and trade systems	Primitive, inferior and miserable whether in animals or economic and trade systems	Primitive, inferior and miserable whether in animals or economic and trade systems	Advanced and superior whether in animals or economic and trade systems
Track Record	lousy in animals, but conservatives are proud of their records	lousy in animals, but liberals are proud of their records	Bad in animals; moderates have no record to brag about.	Excellent track records in animals, but has not been explored yet in economics, politics and trade
Development Stage	Old age stage in animals, economics, politics and trade	Old age stage in animals, economics, politics and trade	Old age stage in animals, economics, politics and trade	Most recent in animal evolution; Will enter infancy stage in economics, politics and trade soon

Table 1 (Continued) : Factors You Should Consider to Choose Your Own Species

Factor	Cold-Blooded Species	Hibernating Species	Mixed Species	Warm-Blooded Species
Identity	Clear	Clear	Vague because of mix and compromise	Clear
Academic Disciplines	Typical macroeconomics and current theories of international trade	Typical macroeconomics and current theories of international trade	Typical macroeconomics and current theories of international trade	Bio-economic engineering and other new disciplines from cross-breeding natural and social sciences
Professionals Providing support	Typical economists and politicians	Typical economists and politicians	Typical economists and politicians	A new breed of bio-economic engineers and warm-blooded politicians
Periods of Prosperity	Age of Reptiles for animals, 19th and 20th centuries for humans	Age of Reptiles for animals, 19th and 20th centuries for humans	Age of Reptiles for animals, never prospered for humans	Age of Mammals for animals, new millennium for humans
Time Factor	Time is against them	Time is against them	Time is against them	Time is on their side
Mental Characteristics	Small brains in animals and humans	Small brains in animals and humans	Small brains in animals and humans	Developed brains in animals and humans

Table 1 (Continued) : Factors You Should Consider to Choose Your Own Species

Factor	Cold-Blooded Species	Hibernating Species	Mixed Species	Warm-Blooded Species
Reader's Additional Factors				
Concluding Comments	Conservatives who still insist on cold-bloodedness after revealing the overwhelming biological facts are *mentally sick*	Liberals who still believe that hibernation is the only way to protect humans against cold economic climates are *also mentally sick*	Moderates who still have hope in mixing and reconciling conservative cold-bloodedness with liberal hibernation are *suckers*	Warm-Blooded Reformists will be the *stars of the new millennium*

Table 2: Score of Items to Choose Your Own Species

Name: _____   Date:_____

Self-Exam Time: New Year   Pre-Election

Item	Cold-Blooded Score	Hibernating Score	Mixed Score	Warm-Blooded Score
Biological Applications				
Economic/Political Applications				
Trade Applications				
Biological Principles				
Economic/Political Principles				
Trade Principles				
Biological Advantages				
Economic/Political Advantages				
Trade Advantages				
Biological Disadvantages				
Economic/Political				
Trade Disadvantages				
Biological Environmental Factor				
Economic/Political Environmental				
Trade Environmental Factor				
Biological Body Size Factor				
Economic/Political Size Factor				
Trade Size Factor				
Biological Performance				
Economic/Political Performance				
Trade Performance				
Characteristics of Species				
Track Record				
Development Stage				
Identity				
Academic Disciplines				
Professionals Providing Support				
Periods of Prosperity				
Time Factor				
Mental Characteristics				
Reader's Additional Factors				
Concluding Comments				
Final Score				

Final Reptilian Score = Final Cold-Blooded Score + Final Hibernating Score + Final Mixed Score = _____

Total Points = Final Reptilian Score + Final Warm-Blooded Score

Final Reptilian Score (%) = 100 x (Final Reptilian Score) / (Total Points) =_____

Final Warm-Blooded Score (%) = 100 x (Final Warm-Blooded Score) / (Total Points) = _____

To simplify things in documenting your results, the final scores of the first three species (cold-blooded, hibernating and mixed) in Table 2 are added together as a single reptilian score. In addition to simplifying things, this will make the score distribution of most conservatives and liberals fairly consistent and easier to compare. On the other hand, the warm-blooded score will have to be separate from the reptilian one. After all, the newly evolving warm-blooded species will have to follow the footsteps of warm-blooded animals as they separate themselves into the two new classes of mammals and birds that are clearly distinguished from the reptile class.

Whether you mentally belong at present to the reptile class or the mammal class in economics and politics, you need to follow the procedure explained in the last four lines of Table 2 to convert your reptilian and warm-blooded scores to percentage points.

As you may have guessed, the last two lines on Table 2 will give the final answer to the examination of your own species. The species that corresponds to the highest score is the species you would like both yourself and our economic and political systems to be. If your reptilian score is higher, then you mentally belong to *Class Reptilia* in your economic and political beliefs. If your warm-blooded score is the winner, then you mentally belong to the *Mammal Class* in economics and politics.

Monitor Your Own Evolution

Many physicians use charts to monitor the progress of their patients over time, especially for critical cases. You should do the same and use charts to monitor the progress of your mental health in economics and politics. You will find out that your reptilian and mammalian scores will not be constant all the time. On the contrary, they will vary from year to year. It may be a good idea if you plot your scores over the years.

Figure 1 will help you plot the results of choosing your own species. As you plot your results, you can look objectively at your evolution from reptilian to warm-blooded form. Every year you will add an additional point to the plot and connect it with the previous year with a straight line. Table 3 should help you organize your records. In this table, you will write down the

Table 3: Documenting the Yearly Results of Choosing Your
          Own Species

Name: _____

Year	Self-Exam Type	Reptilian Score	Warm-Blooded Score
2000	Presidential Election		
2001	New Millennium (Official Date)		
2002	New Year		
	Mid-term Election		
	Average		
2003	New Year		
2004	New Year		
	Presidential Election		
	Average		
2005	New Year		
2006	New Year		
	Mid-term Election		
	Average		
2007	New Year		
2008	New Year		
	Presidential Election		
	Average		
2009	New Year		
2010	New Year		
	Mid-term Election		
	Average		
2011	New Year		
2012	New Year		
	Presidential Election		
	Average		

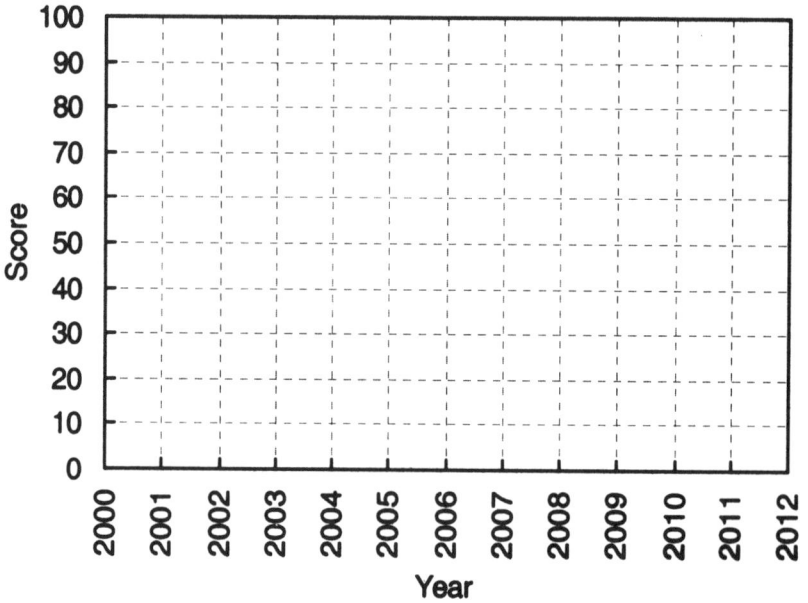

Figure 1: Blank Chart for Plotting Trend of Reptilian and Warm-Blooded Scores for Choosing Your Own Species

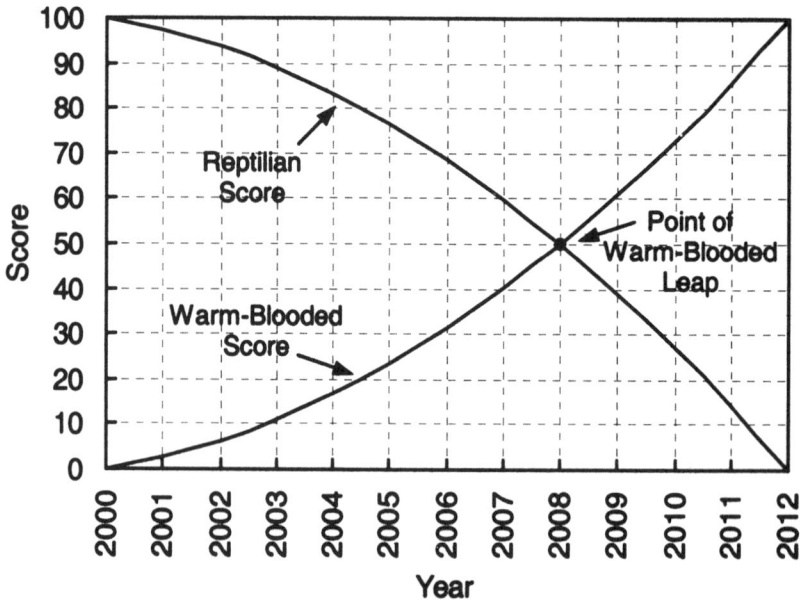

Figure 2: Expected Trend of Reptilian and Warm-Blooded Scores for Typical Conservatives and Liberals

reptilian and warm-blooded score for the New Year Eve's and election day self-exams and average the score of both.

Figure 2 shows an example of what typical conservatives and liberals may encounter as they plot their results. This figure will give you the opportunity to compare your evolution with the expected median trend of most people. As shown in Figure 2, typical conservatives and liberals will start with a high reptilian score and a low warm-blooded one. Over the years, they will have more doubts about their belief in cold-blooded conservatism and hibernating liberalism. At the same time they will be more open to warm-bloodedness. These mental developments will reflect in their scores of the choice of reptilian versus warm-blooded species. Thus, the reptilian scores will gradually sink and the warm-blooded scores will rise.

As shown in Figure 2, both the reptilian line and the warm-blooded line will eventually intersect at some point in the future. That point will have a special meaning as it will mark the leap of your own species from reptilian to warm-blooded form in economic and political beliefs. Your reptilian mentality will *die* and a new warm-blooded mentality will be born. The year corresponding to this critical change will be the most important year in your descendants' family tree. That particular year will mark the last time when your descendants would encounter a link in their family tree with class reptilia! And you will be the only one to take full credit for terminating such a reptilian link and starting a new mammalian link!

The trend of the reptilian line and warm-blooded line shown in Figure 2 is applicable to every single person if given unlimited time. This trend should happen to famous names in economics and politics as well as ordinary people. The only difference that will distinguish different individuals is the slope of both reptilian and warm-blooded lines and when their intersection point takes place. And this is influenced only by intelligence and common sense, and has nothing to do with economic and political fame.

Some smart individuals will digest the warm-blooded message immediately and will take the warm-blooded leap the first year they hear about it. Other individuals will be much slower to respond. After they hear the warm-blooded message, they may be convinced only one percent. Bit by bit over the long years, they will evolve from reptilian to warm-blooded mentality. Such evolution may take ten, twenty or forty years. Still, they will have a chance of witnessing the leap from reptilian to mammalian forms during their lives.

On the other hand, other people will never see their final warm-blooded evolution. Those are too slow and too stubborn. As Thomas Jefferson said, they *are more disposed to suffer than to right themselves by abolishing the (reptilian) forms to which they are accustomed!*

Those people may need hundreds or even thousands of years to be convinced to abandon reptilism and choose warm-bloodedness. Obviously, they will not live that long. They will simply die as reptilian species either in the cold-blooded conservative form or the hibernating liberal form. Before their death they may show no progress, not even being partially convinced by warm-bloodedness. Those stubborn people will never see the warm-blooded salvation in their economic and political mentality during their life. On the positive side, the salvation will happen to their children.

Whether you are smart enough to digest the warm-blooded message quickly in just several years or you need tens, hundreds or thousands of years, you should do your homework to evaluate the choice of your own species. It would be nice if you help people you care about evaluate their species too (you may copy and distribute Tables 1-3 and Figures 1-2 to them). You will need an hour scanning Table 1 and documenting the results on Table 2. You should also monitor the progress of your evolution from reptilian to mammalian forms over the years and plot the results on Figure 1.

Before you finally document these records, close your eyes and try to picture what your descendants will think about you as you choose your own species. Try to squeeze your brain so hard, but not to the point of bursting, to figure out whether your species should be *cold-blooded, hibernating, mixed* or *warm-blooded*. Think about how your descendants will look back at you as the last survivor from *The Dark Age of Reptilian Economics and Politics*. You will be special to them as you will represent their *last link with class reptilia.* And you will be the only one in your family tree who will set the pace of economic and political evolution from reptilian to warm-blooded forms!

You have a golden opportunity no one else ever had or will have—neither your ancestors nor your descendants! If you make the right choice, all your descendants will look appreciatively at you. If you misuse this opportunity, you will make a fool of yourself and your descendents will be ashamed of you. Before you make your final decision of whether *to stick to class reptilia* or to *leap to the mammal class*, try to visualize how you want your descendants to look at you as you *choose your own species.*

PART FOUR

WHAT TO DO NEXT?

13
Declaring War

One great mistake made by *intelligent* people is to refuse to believe that the world (of economics and politics) is as *stupid* as it is.

Mme De Tencin (1771)

An invasion of armies can be resisted, but not an idea whose time has come.

Victor Hugo (1852)

The *truth* is a *bomb*.

Newt Gingrich (1994)

It is tempting to give up or to start to play the (same) game. After all, what is the use of sophisticated thinking or careful examination of the facts if simplistic ideas win every time?

One answer is simply that *it would be wrong to give up*. If the people with good ideas do not *fight* for them, they have no right to complain about the outcome.[1]

Paul Krugman (1994)

We Must Fight the Reptilian Species

Now we've understood the true nature of the reptilian species that rule the world of economics and politics, the next logical step is to decide what we should do about them. Should we continue as usual and accept belonging to class reptilia in our economic and political systems? Or should we break this shameful reality, bring an end to the *Dark Age of Reptilian Economics and Politics* and define a new beginning for the *Bright Age of Mammalian Economics and Politics?*

If we choose to continue to be a part of class reptilia, all we have to do is to do nothing. We let the reptilian species in the Republican and Democratic Parties carry on doing exactly what they currently do. This passive choice may seem easy at first glance. In reality, however, it is not. It is hard because we have to fight with ourselves and with our biological nature which demands that we should belong to warm-blooded economic and political system, not reptilian one. Fighting our internal warm-blooded and mammalian nature should be harder and more painful than fighting our external reptilian enemies.

If we can't accept fighting our own warm-blooded nature— and no genuine human being should accept it—then the only choice left is to *declare war* against the reptilian economic and political species. We shouldn't expect any peaceful settlements between warm-bloodedness and reptilism in the world of economics and politics. Mammals and reptiles have never had peace between them. Neither have good and evil.

Before we declare war, however, we must be aware that the reptilian economic and political species are as vicious as the reptilian species in the movies, *Jurassic Park* and *The Lost World*. Unlike in the movies, courage and good luck won't be enough to win the battle. We need more than that, because our reptilian enemies are numerous, powerful and ferocious. They exist everywhere and control everything in academia, politics and the media. They will strike viciously when their survival is threatened.

If we are serious about fighting reptilian species, we must organize ourselves in a new army called the *Warm-Blooded Army*. In order to win the intellectual war, the Warm-Blooded Army must think, plan and act like any military army of an advanced nation.

List of the Reptilian Enemies

Before any army goes to the battlefield, it needs a list of the enemy troops, how they are distributed and where they are located. We need a similar list of our enemies, the reptilian economic and political species, and how and where they hide. This list includes these two major groups:

1. Economists, professors of economics, council of economic advisors of the president, governors and chairman of the Federal Reserve Board and other authorities in economics. All these professionals were trained in reptilian economic theories. They must be intellectually defeated and replaced by new breeds of professionals called bio-economic engineers.

2. *Republican and Democratic Parties and their members*: This list includes big names such as President Clinton, current members of Congress, and all political candidates running for the year 2000 election, both conservative and liberal.

List of the Warm-Blooded Army's Troops

In addition to preparing a list of our enemies, we need to prepare another list of our troops. Like any modern army, the list of the Warm-Blooded Army's troops will include two categories: the *fighting troops* and the *technical troops*. Soldiers of the fighting troops will fight intellectually by sending the message of warm-bloodedness individually to everyone they know in their communities, at work and in their neighborhoods. The technical troops will train the fighting troops and provide them with the most recent, most advanced and most effective intellectual weapons.

The fighting troops of any conventional army includes four types: infantry, airborne, mechanized and armored. Similarly, the fighting troops of the Warm-Blooded Army will feature four types of troops that will complement each other. These types are:

1. *People fed up* with Republicans, Democrats, politicians, economists, free trade proponents, protectionists and their inability to solve our problems. The fighters of this group will

turn their negative feelings into something positive, namely fighting the evil reptilian species until they go extinct.

2. *Moderates, Independents, and Reformists* who seek to achieve new warm-blooded identity in economics and politics.

3. *Bored individuals* who are turned off by the repeated, boring talks in economics and politics and are looking for more exciting and sophisticated ways of thinking.

4. *Caring individuals* who believe that we must not allow reptilian species to control the future of this nation.

Unlike conventional armies where soldiers are typically specialized, the Warm-Blooded Army will feature fighters belonging to more than one troop type. In fact, a big chunk of the fighters of the Warm-Blooded Army will belong to all the above four types. This will provide more skills, flexibility and intellectual maneuverability.

In order to support and train the fighting troops with the most advanced intellectual weapons, the Warm-Blooded Army will feature the following nine types of technical troops:

1. *Engineers* seeking new intellectual opportunities in economics and politics, such as how to design and improve economic thermostats that apply the concept of automatic feedback control. Many will like to contribute to the new discipline of bio-economic engineering that will compete against the reptilian version called macroeconomics. Others will explore how to achieve six sigma quality in economics and politics.

2. *Biologists* seeking to generalize the classification of animals according to cold-bloodedness, hibernation and warm-bloodedness to the classification of economic and political species. Many biologists will join to assume new economic and political responsibilities. They will have fun teaming with engineers to invade the habitats of economics and politics and expand their professional territories.

3. *Information systems experts* who will design new government systems based on *direct electronic democracy* in which citizens may bypass politicians during voting on different issues whenever they feel like. They will simply sign on their home computer and send their votes directly to the web site of the Congress.

4. *Thinkers, philosophers, scientists and social scientists* who will be interested in the concept and practice of bridging natural sciences with social sciences in the new discipline of bio-economic engineering and other disciplines that will follow. They will study how the Warm-Blooded Army uses them as advanced weapons of mass destruction in the war against reptilian species.

5. *Comedians, artists and cartoonists* who will be looking at wonderful business opportunities to be had from picking on the stupid species that currently rule the world of economics and politics.

6. *Military strategists and tacticians* who would like to apply their expertise to define the overall mission, strategy and tactics of the Warm-Blooded Army. They will recognize that the cultural war against reptilian economics and politics is more important than any other war in history. It is more fun too.

7. *Private firms* that will develop and market business cycle thermostats, trade thermostats and any other needed economic thermostat: These firms will be looking for exploring new markets for their new thermostat products. As spending on the intellectual weapons of the Warm-Blooded Army increases, the sales and profits of those firms will boom.

8. *Economists* who are not satisfied with what is going on in economics. While about 90 percent of economists will be on the list of enemies, the remaining 10 percent will join the Warm-Blooded Army and will cooperate with the rest of the technical groups. Although they will be called traitors by their old colleagues, they will find satisfaction in changing their career from typical economists to bio-economic engineers.

9. Politicians who are not satisfied with the current practice of politics in which the rules of winning are based on deceiving and fooling the common people rather than looking objectively at the facts.

All the above nine types of technical troops must work harmoniously with each other and with the other four fighting troops. After all they have a common goal.

With the impressive list of the fighting and technical troops, it will only be a matter of a few years before the Warm-Blooded Army will have all it needs to become as well-organized, well-equipped and well-trained as any modern army. In addition, its fighting and technical troops will be enormously motivated and enjoy high morale. Above all, every man and woman in this army will be looking for the opportunity to be remembered in history as one of the heroes that exterminated the reptilian species in the world of economics and politics and thus provided a peaceful environment for warm-blooded species to grow, multiply and prosper.

Ranks in the Warm-Blooded Army

In any organization, people must be ranked according to their talents, skills and other abilities. Those who score the highest should be the leaders. Others will be the followers. We need something similar in the Warm-Blooded Army. The ranking process, however, should not be too authoritarian, rigid or bureaucratic. Instead, it should be simple, flexible and adaptive.

A proposal for the ranking process is to have every person joining the Warm-Blooded Army in either the fighting or technical troops start at the level of *warm-blooded fighter*. Above this introductory level, there will be five higher levels: *sergeant, lieutenant, captain, colonel* and *general*.

Every warm-blooded fighter should register upon joining the Warm-Blooded Army. Registration will serve three purposes. The first is to establish census data to let the public know the number of fighters in the Warm-Blooded Army and their growth from month to month and from year to year. The second purpose is to establish an official record for fighters indicating the date they joined the Warm-Blooded Army. Moreover, any new fighter should write on the registration form the name of the person who has delivered the warm-blooded message to him or her. Every time a warm-blooded fighter persuades a person to join the Warm-Blooded Army, a point will be added to his or her achievement record. These points will determine how fighters in the Warm-Blooded Army get promoted to higher ranks.

If a fighter scores 10 points (which means he or she has added 10 new fighters to the Warm-Blooded Army), he or she will be promoted to the level of warm-blooded sergeant. Attaining a higher level will require more points. A warm-blooded lieutenant, captain, colonel and general will need 100, 1000, 10,000 and 100,000 points respectively.

Still, those top-ranking officials start from the bottom as fighters. Following such a humble start, any average person can advance to the level of warm-blooded sergeant with a reasonable amount of effort. All you have to do is to approach 15 to 20 persons hoping to convince 10 of them to open their eyes to the current reptilian reality and the need to seek new, warm-blooded economic and political solutions. That may not be too hard if you have the ability to persuade others and work sincerely for our good cause. In fact, promotion to a level of sergeant in the Warm-Blooded Army is much easier and much faster than that in a typical army. Motivated fighters can reach this level in just a few months.

Promotion to the level of warm-blooded lieutenant requires someone who is very active in the community and persistent, so that he or she can send the warm-blooded message to at least 150 persons. The higher levels of captain, colonel or general would need more than communication skills, motivation and being active. The person needs to be a famous public figure, a celebrity or an extraordinary achiever. These positions, therefore, will be relatively few.

People in the Warm-Blooded Army should not be too much occupied with reaching higher levels. Most of the fighting, especially at the beginning of the intellectual war, will be done on the levels of fighters, sergeants and lieutenants. Because there will be many of them, they will achieve most of the results. Once we see significant figures of higher levels, we will know for sure that the war against reptilism is almost over.

The Warm-Blooded Army of each nation will be headed by a *warm-blooded commander-in-chief*, who will be elected by the entire army. This position will symbolize the unity of the army, although fighters will have no obligation to follow exactly what the commander-in-chief envisions. Still this position is important, as the person in charge will have the responsibility of defining the overall mission of the Warm-Blooded Army, its strategy and tactics.

Since the war against reptilism will be all over the world, it will be useful to have all Warm-Blooded Armies united. To achieve this, all the warm-blooded commanders-in-chief of different nations will elect a single person to lead them. Such a person will be called *worldwide warm-blooded commander-in-chief*. Again, this leadership position is more symbolic rather executive. The majority of decisions that define the mission, strategy and tactics of each nation will be done at the rank of the warm-blooded commander-in-chief of that particular nation. The worldwide warm-blooded commander-in-chief should not interfere in little details of the war against reptilism that may vary according to different circumstances of different nations.

The author's firm *Kammelosaur Warm-Blooded Research* will volunteer to establish and maintain a computerized database for the registration to the U.S. Warm-Blooded Army and for calculating the number of points for promotion to higher ranks. The newcomers to the Warm-Blooded Army need to fill out the form on pages 205-206 and mail it to the attached address at the bottom of the second page. You need not pay any fee to register. You may copy the registration form and distribute it to any number of individuals. You may also attach the form to your web site, add your name in the Referral Credit section, and let others download it. By approaching individuals through the Internet or face to face, you can persuade quite a few of them to join the Warm-Blooded Army.

Kammelosaur Warm-Blooded Research Inc will send free of charge a certificate of joining the army and of promotion to the level of warm-blooded sergeant and above to anyone who accumulates the needed points.

Kammelosaur Warm-Blooded Research Inc will continue to assume the responsibility of maintaining the records of the Warm-Blooded Army and issuing certificates of membership. The author's firm will continue serving the army as long as the troops are happy with our service. If for any reason the majority of

APPLICATION FOR JOINING THE WARM-BLOODED ARMY

Name: _____

Address: _____

_____

I acknowledge that the current economic and political species that rule this nation and determine the future of our children belong mentally to class reptilia. I realize the need to fight these reptilian species so that we can deliver warm-blooded economics and politics to our nation and our children.

I understand that the fight against the reptilian species will be only intellectual, using ideas, reasoning and thinking within democratic principles. There will be no tolerance for physical violence. I will obey all the laws and fight according to the highest moral and ethical standards. I realize that if I am involved in any physical violence or misconduct, I will be expelled immediately from the Warm-Blooded Army.

Mark appropriate technical skills' box if interested in joining the Technical troops:

☐ Engineer
☐ Biologist
☐ Warm-blooded politician
☐ Information system expert
☐ Thinker/philosopher/scientist/social scientist
☐ Comedian/artist/cartoonist
☐ Military strategist/tactician
☐ Economist willing to become bio-economic engineer
☐ Employee of a firm planning to market economic thermostats
☐ Other technical competence or talent not listed above, but may be considered for future technical troops. Please specify:

_____

_____

_____

Referral Credit

I heard about the Warm-Blooded Army through:
☐ Personal Contact   ☐ Media Contact

If heard through media, indicate name of media:

_____

Type of media: ☐ Newspaper ☐ Magazine ☐ Book ☐ Radio
☐ TV

Person to whom I would like to give credit for convincing me to
join the Warm-Blooded Army:

Name: _____

City:_____ State: _____

**Personal Information for providing overall statistical data about
the troops of the Warm-Blooded Army** (Filling out this part is
optional)

Age: ☐ Less than 20   ☐ 20-29   ☐ 30-39   ☐ 40-49   ☐ 50-64
☐ 65 and above

Sex: ☐ Male   ☐ Female

Previous political background:
☐ Moderate/Independent/Reformist
☐ Conservative
☐ Liberal
☐ Never participated in or was serious about politics

Signature:_____ Date: _____

Mail this form to: Kammelosaur Warm-Blooded Research
PO Box 2119, Peabody, MA 01960

people in the army prefer to have an independent organization to assume these responsibilities, we will pass the records to the new organization. After all, warm-bloodedness is our business. And we care about the Warm-Blooded Army and believe it deserves the highest level of service by us or others.

War Objective

Fighters of the Warm-Blooded Army must have a clear overall objective that needs to be followed despite distractions. Without clarity of objective there is no basis for fighting.

The overall objective (or mission) of the Warm-Blooded Army is to defeat the reptilian enemy's armed forces in the three frontiers of *academia*, *media* and *politics*. This will end of the rule of class reptilia over humans in their economic and political systems. We want to win the war against reptilism as well as the peace that will follow. This means that we must completely destroy the reptilian enemies so that they will never be able to fight again.

Some military theorists assert that wars can be won without destroying the enemy's armed forces and that the proper overall objective should be the destruction of the enemy's ability and will to resist. While there is controversy about the validity of such an objective in conventional wars, it is definitely not suitable in the war against the reptilian economic and political enemies. Our war will be more vicious. We shouldn't look for anything less than the complete destruction of all reptilian troops. This means complete destruction of the Republican and Democratic parties and replacing them by the Warm-Blooded Reform Party. It means also complete destruction of macroeconomics and existing theories of international trade and replacing them with bio-economic engineering. Obviously, the latter means destroying most typical economists and replacing them by bio-economic engineers.

This overall mission may not be achieved in a single battle. Therefore, we need an incremental objective for each battle or each time frame. For example, an incremental objective is to have 5 percent (or even 2 percent) more of the population join the Warm-Blooded Army every year. This may seem like a humble or slow incremental objective. But it is not that bad compared to the time major changes in human history take. What is more important is that the incremental objective should be attainable. If we increase public support by just 2 percent every year, we can get very close to the overall objective of complete destruction of the reptilian forces in economics and politics in just two decades.

War Strategy

The strategy of a conventional army may be defined as "the art and science of employing the armed forces of a nation to secure the objects of national policy by the application of force or the threat of force."

The Warm-Blooded Army needs to define its strategy like any conventional army. We can make use of the above definition after making some adjustments to account for the fact that fighting in the Warm-Blooded Army is *intellectual, not physical*. Then the strategy of the Warm-Blooded Army becomes "*the art and science of employing the warm-blooded armed forces—in both fighting and technical troops—to secure the objectives of the army's mission and vision in economics and politics by the application of intellectual force or the threat of intellectual force.*"

Since wars can be won decisively only by taking the offensive, the strategy of the Warm-Blooded Army must provide for the continuous development and maintenance of the fighting and technical troops in sufficient numbers and suitable types to conduct offensive intellectual operations on a large scale. A strategist in a typical army is usually confronted with the task of deciding which troops must be maintained actively and which can be deferred yet mobilized and equipped in time to meet the strategy. A strategist in the Warm-Blooded Army will have to be different. He or she must maintain all the troops fully active all the time.

The general forms of strategic offensive actions in typical wars are *penetration, envelopment, double envelopment, turning movement* and *pursuit*. Out of these major five offensive strategies, three will be suitable for the fight against reptilian economics and politics: *penetration, double envelopment* and *pursuit*.

Penetration means using concentrated intellectual forces at one or more localities to pierce the reptilian enemy line so that more forces can penetrate further. Double envelopment will attack the two *left and right rear ends* of the reptilian enemies in order to cut their supplies. Penetration and double envelopment will force the reptilian enemies to fight in several directions, at once. To maximize the effectiveness of penetration and double envelopment, they should be followed by pursuit in which the defeated reptilian forces are pursued relentlessly and intellectually captured or defeated.

The most important part of the *penetration strategy* is to select a point in the enemy's front line that is *relatively weak* and has an *important strategic location* which can serve as a new base for future attacks. We should do the same in our fight against reptilian economics and politics. We need to find out which point on the economic and political battlefield is most vulnerable to our attack and would serve as a new base for organizing more troops. Should it be the left, middle or the right?

Conservatives put a lot of defensive troops and ammunition in the right wing territories of economics and politics. They don't care about the middle. Similarly, liberals favor the left wing territories and don't care about the middle either. Both conservatives and liberals consider the middle of the economic and political battlefield as a rural area that belongs to neither of them. This makes the middle the most vulnerable area. Conservatives and liberals don't realize that the middle, which has been the least important territory during *The Age of Reptilian Economics and Politics,* will turn out to be the most important strategic base during the coming war between warm-bloodedness and reptilism.

A good example of how the middle is ignored is the CNN program *Crossfire.* The program features hosts and guests from the *right* representing *cold-blooded conservatism.* It also features hosts and guests from the *left* representing *hibernating liberalism.* The program tries to be fair in balancing the presentation of both left and right views. Unfortunately, it presents no host nor guest from the middle—no Independent or Reformist. It ignores the middle completely as if it does not exist. It seems that the producers of *Crossfire* think of the middle as a vague mix of cold-blooded conservatism and hibernating liberalism, not worthy of presentation. They have to realize that the middle is where the new warm-blooded economic and political species will evolve and rise. The producers of *Crossfire* and other media programs must change their perception if they want to continue to attract intelligent viewers.

Many moderates, Independents and Reformists feel angry and betrayed by the current simplistic views of the media that inflate the importance of the cold-blooded right and hibernating left and ignore the warm-blooded middle. There are many people dwelling in the middle and they probably outnumber both conservatives and liberals lumped together. They are often treated as second-class by the media and reptilian politicians.

The Warm-Blooded Army cannot ask for a more wonderful opportunity. The middle is so weak and vulnerable. The people in the middle are fed up. Many feel too insulted to choose between cold-blooded conservatism and hibernating liberalism and therefore do not show up at elections at all as they do not expect any victory for a third party.

People in the middle will not have to suffer anymore if the Warm-Blooded Army invades their territories and delivers them from the evils and hardships of reptilian economics and politics. Not only will they welcome the Warm-Blooded Army, but they will also join its troops. With more troops, the Warm-Blooded Army can secure its new bases at the strategic middle and then proceed to invade more territories.

After the offensive strategy of *penetration* at the middle is successfully completed, the Warm-Blooded Army will strike a *double envelopment attack* at the right and left wings of the economic and political battlefield. The mission of the right wing attack is to prove to typical conservatives that there are more genuine conservative values in warm-blooded economics and politics than in typical cold-blooded conservatism. For example, warm-blooded governments will replace discretion of politicians, bureaucrats and the Federal Reserve Board in setting economic policies by economic and trade thermostats. This will make future warm-blooded governments smaller in size and power than any conservative government in history.

The attack on the left wing will be similar. It will show typical liberals that there are more genuine liberal values in warm-blooded economics and politics than in typical hibernating liberalism. For example, warm-blooded economic systems will help the poor, the middle and working classes more than any liberal government in history.

In addition to planning the attack from the middle and proceeding to the right and left territories, strategy will involve planning a sequence of further attacks in politics, media and academia. For maximum effectiveness, we should start at the weakest of these three frontiers. The weak spot is politics because it involves moderates, Independents and Reformists who are ignored and abused the most. The best strategy, therefore, should start by emphasizing the political side, attacking the Republican and Democratic Parties and their ideologies. This attack will be announced by proclaiming the birth of a new Warm-Blooded version of the current Reform Party.

After launching the attack on the political side, it will be time for applying increased pressure on the media to attract their attention to the Warm-Blooded Reform Party and the Warm-Blooded Army. The media will have to eventually yield to the pressure if a significant number of the public becomes receptive to the views of the warm-blooded economics and politics. The media are influenced by firms that own the newspapers, magazines, radio and TV stations. Most of these firms care about revenue that comes from their audience rather than from endorsement of specific political views or causes. If the top executives of these firms discover that recognizing the Warm-Blooded Reform Party and the Warm-Blooded Army will increase their profits, they will recognize them and give them fair representation.

The most difficult fight will be against academia. The academic territories will include professors of macroeconomics who cling more to the past and present and lack a vision of the future. They assume the future is just a mere extension of the reptilian past and present. Dealing with these species will be difficult as they will be the last to yield to the intellectual attacks of the Warm-Blooded Army. They will have to see enormous victories along the territories of politics and the media before they accept bio-economic engineering and other disciplines that will be born from crossbreeding natural and social sciences. It is a pity that the species that are supposed to be one of the smartest—college professors of economics—will be the last to surrender to the intellectual attacks of the Warm-Blooded Army. It is ironic that ordinary people and the media will get the warm-blooded message faster.

In brief, the strategy of the Warm-Blooded Army will involve direct penetration at the middle of the political battlefield followed by double envelopment attacks at the right and left wing territories. These attacks will emphasize the political side first, and then proceed to the media and then finally to the academia. As the reptilian enemies retreat, the warm-blooded troops will follow them closely with more terrorizing actions to increase their demoralization and disorganization and give them no opportunity to recover or reorganize. At that time, the Warm-Blooded Army will strike viciously with the pursuit strategy to intellectually capture the retreating reptilian troops and wipe them out completely from existence in economics and politics!

War Tactics

In addition to strategy, the Warm-Blooded Army must plan its tactics. The distinction between strategy and tactics has often been explained by prominent military writers. Field Marshal Earl Wavell said: "Tactics is the art of handling troops on the battlefield; strategy is the art of bringing forces to the battlefield in a favorable position." General Sir Edward B. Hamley said: "The theater of war is the province of strategy; the field of battles is the province of tactics." And General von Clausewitz said: "Tactics is the art of using troops in the battle; strategy is the art of using battles to win the war."

It is difficult in practice to distinguish tactics from strategy because the two are closely interdependent. Indeed in the twentieth century, tactics have been termed *operational strategy*.

In the war against reptilian economics and politics, strategy plans how to place and maneuver the troops of the Warm-Blooded Army in the economic and political battlefield so as to bring them into combat under the most advantageous conditions possible. Strategy also involves planning how to maneuver the troops along the three frontiers of politics, media and academia to achieve the best results. On the other hand, tactics is the art of using fighting troops, technical troops and intellectual weapons in combat against the reptilian enemy.

Tactics employed by individual technical troops are called *minor tactics*. The commander of each technical troop—such as engineering or biology—will be responsible for defining the *minor mission* of that technical troop and how to accomplish it through minor tactics. On the other hand, tactics of the technical troops as a whole are called *grand tactics*. These will be under the responsibility of the warm-blooded commander-in-chief of each army. In addition, he or she must define the overall mission and how to maximize *tactical mobility* to achieve it. Tactical mobility is the ability to move intellectual weapons rapidly from technical troops to the fighting troops.

An important grand tactic is to utilize the hostility between conservatives and liberals. Conservatives and liberals have been enemies for as along as they have been in existence. Many conservatives love to laugh at the simplistic mentality of hibernating liberalism, and use such attacks to prove that cold-blooded conservatism makes more sense. It will be a tactical advantage for the warm-blooded fighters to join conservatives as they attack liberals.

By the same token, many liberals love to attack the naïve mentality of cold-blooded conservatism, and use such attacks to prove that hibernating liberalism makes more sense. The warm-blooded fighters can join liberals in their attacks against conservatives.

By joining conservatives as they strike liberals and by joining liberals as they strike conservatives, the Warm-Blooded Army should be able to cause severe intellectual damage along the defense lines of both conservative and liberal ideologies and doctrines!

The Barking and Biting Tactic

This tactic was used successfully by Newt Gingrich to win a Republican House majority in 1994 after more than sixty years of Democratic control. To apply this tactic in our war, the tactician team should plan the following steps:

1) Identify suitable timing: While Gingrich selected the intermediate election year 1994 (as he was concentrating on winning House seats), it would be more advantageous for the Warm-Blooded tacticians to target a presidential election year, such as the year 2004 or 2008. We may not have enough time to apply this tactic in the year 2000 presidential election, although it would be a wonderful opportunity to do so.

2) Identify a list of inferior and awful things in reptilian economics and politics and describe them to people with a simplistic mentality using the most negative words one may find in a thesaurus. Examples of the words Gingrich used are *pathetic, sick, traitors, incompetent, anti-flag, anti-family, anti-child, corrupt, disgrace, bizarre and obsolete.* The purpose is to arouse emotions rather than explain the facts! In our war against reptilism, we need to modify this tactic a little bit. We shouldn't fight with vague and overused words like what Gingrich did, but we need to explore other new biological words that not only would arouse emotions of individuals with a simplistic mentality but also stimulate the intellect of those with sophisticated mentality. Examples of these new words are *reptilism, reptilian, cold-blooded, hibernating, inferior and primitive economic and political species and walnut-sized brains.*

3) Train the politicians who are interested in applying this tactic aimed at arousing emotions how to bark loudly and bite viciously like mad dogs, once they are unleashed in the election campaign! The training will feature watching and studying live beasts in addition to video tapes of the most savage animals. Then, the instructor will ask the trainees to forget that they are civilized humans and that they need to imitate savage animals following the *BB (Barking and Biting) Tactic.* It may be helpful to starve the trainees for a few days and then throw them big chunks of raw meat—a whole leg, a shoulder or a whole carcass—on the floor. Then, they visualize their political enemies in the place of the dead meat and practice the barking and biting tactic. Because the trainees will make a tremendous noise in such a visualization technique, the training facilities should be located in remote, uninhabited

areas. This way, the possibility of a costly lawsuit from annoyed neighbors may be avoided.

4) Publish a positive, revolutionary agenda in the form of an appealing *Contract with America*. This positive part will bring some balance to the negative part involving barking and biting. Just as the negative tactic should be modified to suit the needs of the Warm-Blooded Army, the positive tactic must be tailored as well. To do so, the Warm-Blooded tacticians must give a unique name to their agenda book, a name like *The Warm-Blooded Contract with America* to distinguish it from the earlier conservative version of the year 1994 that actually meant *The Cold-Blooded Reptilian Contract with America,* and from the possibility of a similar liberal version of a *Hibernating Contract with America.*

5) Once the new Warm-Blooded Contract is published and interested politicians are trained in barking and biting, they will be unleashed and their jaws will be unrestrained! Timing of this event should be carefully selected, something like a few months before the target presidential election. At that moment the warm-blooded politicians will strike viciously like mad dogs attacking their reptilian enemies!

While the original Newt Gingrich tactic proved successful in 1994, many political critics dislike it because it is too savage and involves too much political barking, biting, noise and viciousness. They argue that political fights should feature more decency and more sense. This argument, however, is more idealistic than practical. In the political jungle, winning is more important than anything else. What good do decency and making sense do to an unelected politician without a job?

Despite its indecency and nonsense, the Newt Gingrich's barking and biting tactic must be considered seriously—after proper modifications—by the leadership of the Warm-Blooded Army. After all, it has an extremely great potential. To maximize this potential, the leader-ship should try to persuade Gingrich to provide a consultation service on how to apply the biting and barking tactic and on how to write a new *Warm-Blooded Contract with America for the New Millennium,* a contract that will be treasured by all future generations till the end of time!

Building the Reptilian Armies

The invasion of the economic and political territories by the troops of the Warm-Blooded Army will scare both conservatives and liberals, especially after a successful strike using the *Newt Gingrich's Barking and Biting Tactic*. They will panic as they see many people exiting the Republican and Democratic Parties to join the Warm-Blooded Reform Party and the Warm-Blooded Army.

But conservatives and liberals will not stand still watching the Warm-Blooded Army wipe them out of existence. They will call for the defense of reptilian economics and politics by establishing two armies: the *Cold-Blooded Army* featuring conservative troops and the *Hibernating Army* featuring liberal troops. Both armies will have similar ranking structure as the Warm-Blooded Army. The troops will basically include *cold-blooded (or hibernating) fighters*. Above such basic levels, there will be five higher levels of *sergeant, lieutenant, captain* and *general*. Each army will be headed by *a commander-in-chief*.

Building and organizing the ranking structures of the Cold-Blooded Army and the Hibernating Army will add a new element of hostility. It will heat up the war between the new warm-blooded middle on one side and the cold-blooded right and hibernating left on the other side. This will raise the war to the high level of hostility that was experienced between reptiles and mammals during the end of the Age of Reptiles!

Unification of Cold-Bloodedness and Hibernation

As the Warm-Blooded Army strikes more viciously on the Cold-Blooded Army and the Hibernating Army, both reptilian armies will try to think up a new fighting strategy. If they fight separately, without mutual coordination or cooperation, they will definitely lose. They will need, therefore, to cease their hostility toward each other. They must go even one step further and consolidate their fighting troops under one army called the *Unified Reptilian Army*.

Troops in the new unified army will have the same ranks. This means cold-blooded fighters and hibernating fighters will unite together under the rank of *reptilian fighters*. Higher unified levels will include *reptilian sergeant, lieutenant, captain, colonel, general* and *commander-in-chief.*

While the unification of the Cold-Blooded Army and the Hibernating Army into the Reptilian Army will seem like a war necessity, many people will be disillusioned by such unification. They will wonder why conservatives and liberals have forgotten their huge differences in values and principles and united to fight the warm-blooded species that are even closer to them than they are to each other! The answer is that while conservatives and liberals are far apart, they are also close in that they belong mentally to the economic and political version of the *reptile class*! The troops of the Warm-Blooded Army belong to a completely different class called the economic and political version of the *mammal class.* The classification according to reptilism and mammalism is more important than classification according to principles, values and ideologies!

While there is an element of logic in this explanation, there is an element of stupidity in the reality itself! Indeed, it would be a great mistake for any logical person to refuse to believe that the current world of economics and politics is as stupid as it really is! And it would be another great mistake not to participate in declaring war against the stupid reptilian species that currently rule the stupid world of economics and politics!

14
The First Battle

The *First blow* is half the battle.

Oliver Goldsmith (1764)

It is not a field of a few acres of ground, but a *cause*, that we are defending, and whether we defeat the enemies in *one battle*, or by degrees, the consequences will be the same.

Thomas Paine (1777)

The *new millennium* should involve a great sense of *discontinuity*. Powerful forces for *upheaval* are converging. Popular willingness to *accept far-reaching changes* should be unusually high. [1]

Kevin Phillips (1994)

Timing of the First Strike

The most critical decision an army takes before it strikes against the enemy is timing the first attack. This decision will have a great influence on war developments. The main advantage of being on the offensive side is that the attacking army will set the time of the first strike for its own advantages. Being on the offensive will boost morale and create an aggressive spirit. The defensive army will have less control, at least during the beginning of the war. It will have to live with the timing of the first strike, whether it likes it or not.

I have been lucky to reveal the *nature of the economic and political species* and their classification according to cold-bloodedness, hibernation and warm-bloodedness around the coming of the new millennium. Following revealing this classification, we need to build and organize the Warm-Blooded Army and make it ready to strike the reptilian enemies in a fierce intellectual war.

This war will be influenced primarily by psychological factors. We need to highlight the positive factors that will boost the morale of the warm-blooded troops. They should know that a new age with new opportunities for new warm-blooded economic and political species is coming. We also need to maximize the negative factors that will depress the morale of the reptilian enemies. They should know that the old age, the last two centuries that have witnessed the rise of reptilism in the world of economics and politics, is coming to an end soon. It would be hard to justify the existence of old, primitive and inferior species that belong to the dark reptilian past in a new age and a new millennium.

What Is Special about the Coming of the New Millennium?

The coming of the new millennium is a unique event; it happens once every thousand years. We should consider ourselves privileged to witness this special event. Our descendants will have to wait about forty generations to witness the new millennium of the year 3000.

The transformation from *The Dark Age of Reptilian Economics and Politics* to *The Bright Age of Mammalian Economics and Politics* will be another unique event in human history. Unlike the new millennium that comes every thousand years, this transformation will come only once in the entire human history. No future generations will ever see something as important and as crucial as this. The mammalian transformation of economics and politics, therefore, will be more special and more striking than the coming of the new millennium.

We, the survivors of the late twentieth century, are very special people. Not only will we have the opportunity to witness the arrival of the third millennium, but we will also see with our own eyes the evolution of economics and politics from reptilian to warm-blooded mammalian form. This will have an everlasting impact on all coming generations, just as the story of the extinction of reptiles and rise of mammals had an impact on the history of life. Fortunately, this great event will happen in a great and special time: the coming of the third millennium. We simply can't ask for more!

Launching the First Battle

An important part of the strategy of the Warm-Blooded Army is to define how the entire war is broken down into a series of battles and then how each battle is broken down into a series of offensive strikes. Each battle will have its own objective, strategy and tactics that should be harmonious with the overall objective, strategy and tactics of the entire war.

The first battle has already started. It would be desirable to end the first and next battles with a memorable date that will have a psychological impact as well. Since the ultimate goal of the war against reptilism is to have one day a *warm-blooded President* walk in victory into the White House and be accompanied by a *warm-blooded Congress,* it will be effective to end each battle on the presidential election day. Then we can evaluate the result of each battle objectively.

This means the first battle extends from the beginning of the year 2000 to the presidential election day of that year. The second battle will start immediately after that and end on the presidential election day of the year 2004. The third battle will start after the second one and end on the presidential election of the year 2008, and so on for the subsequent battles until the war against the reptilian species in economics and politics is over.

Battle Growth

Every human being grows gradually from infancy to childhood, then to the teenage years before the peak during adulthood. The Warm-Blooded Army, too, will grow like a human being as it finishes one battle and moves to the next. The army will live its infancy and childhood during its first battle. It will grow into the teenager state in the second battle and will finally reach its adulthood during the third and following battles.

While the Warm-Blooded Army will grow from infancy to adulthood, the reptilian enemies will gradually age. Reptilism in the Republican and Democratic Parties is right now at old age stage and will get even older as time goes by! The situation is like a fight between a little kid and an old man. The old man may beat the kid badly. But if we wait a few years, the kid will grow stronger as the old man becomes weaker. Eventually, the kid bill be able to beat the old man.

Like a little kid fighting an old man, the Warm-Blooded Army may not be able to impose serious threats to the reptilian enemies during the first battle of the year 200. But as time goes by, the Warm-Blooded Army will become stronger and the reptilian enemies weaker. It is quite possible that the reptilian enemies will be sent to nursing homes before a direct confrontation with the Warm-Blooded Army takes place. Even if they choose not to retire from ruling the world of economics and politics, the Warm-Blooded Army will eventually reach maturity and launch its final strike to wipe them completely from existence.

Objective of the First Battle

An important part of the strategy in typical, long wars is to divide the overall war objective into smaller increments. Each of these increments is just a fraction of the overall objective. A strategist will then assign the different incremental objectives to different battles.

The war against reptilism should be planned like typical, long wars. This requires that the overall objective of complete destruction of the reptilian enemies should be divided into smaller, incremental objectives. Each battle will achieve partial destruction. The combined battles will achieve the total destruction. The partial destruction in each battle—or at least severe weakening of the enemy's forces—must be achieved in each of the frontiers of politics, media and academia.

The objective of the first battle in politics is to convince most Independents and Reformists to seek a new, clear identity in a warm-blooded version of the Reform Party. In addition, we need to persuade the smartest 5 percent of Republicans to abandon the Republican Party because it represents *reptilian cold-bloodedness.* We also need to persuade the smartest 5 percent of Democrats to abandon the Democratic Party because it represents dull *hibernation.* We should not worry at present about the majority of Republicans and Democrats who have modest intelligence. They need several years to understand and digest the warm-blooded message in economics and politics. Even with their huge numbers, they are less important, in the long run, than the few smartest Republicans and Democrats who will immediately abandon their reptilian parties and join the Warm-Blooded Reform Party.

By winning most Independents and Reformists in addition to the smartest 5 percent of conservatives and liberals, the Warm-Blooded Army should easily win at least 30 percent of the total number of registered voters. That will make the year 200 presidential election a very close race between the three sides.

Next to politics, the objective in the media battle is to achieve victory in at least 50 percent of media channels. We must persuade them to abandon their primitive and simplistic views, in which they see economics and politics as either the right wing, left wing, or a vague mix of both. They should open their eyes to see a new, innovative middle representing warm-bloodedness and mammalism.

We are not asking the media to take the side of the warm-blooded middle and be hostile to the cold-blooded right and the hibernating left. They can remain neutral between the three sides. All we are asking is that they recognize the warm-blooded middle and treat it as an equal of the cold-blooded right and the hibernating left. That is not too much to ask. If a media channel fails to recognize the new warm-blooded middle, it will lose many of its smart audience who will not like such unfair practice. And once customers are lost, it will be hard to gain them back, even if media channels correct their earlier mistakes.

Finally, the objective of the battle in academia is to persuade at least 50 percent of professors of engineering and sciences of the potential of bio-economic engineering. In addition, we should target the smartest 5 percent of professors of economics to abandon the current reptilian theories of *macroeconomics* and *international trade*. Then, they can join the professors of engineering and sciences and together they can lay the foundation of bio-economic engineering.

Bio-economic engineering will be the first baby born in a family that will include more offspring from the crossbreeding of natural and social sciences. We should be looking to sell the idea of such crossbreeding to at least 50 percent of professors of sciences and engineering and to 20 percent of professors of social sciences.

The fighters of the Warm-Blooded Army must recognize that achieving the battle objectives in each of the three frontiers of politics, media and academia is equally important. Warm-blooded fighters should not consider the first battle mission as a complete success unless each objective in each frontier is fully accomplished.

Strategy of the First Battle

The strategy of the first battle will have many things in common with the overall strategy of the entire war. A strategist in the Warm-Blooded Army should recognize that while the missions of the three frontiers of politics, media and academia are equally important, fighting will not be equally fierce. The easiest victories can be obtained first in politics. Once the warm-blooded troops occupy more territories in politics, the strategist can move more fighting troops into the frontier of media. Again, once the warm-blooded troops are recognized in more media channels, the strategist will move the troops to conquer the last frontier: academia.

The strategy of looking for easy victories first and then proceeding to the more difficult ones should be applied too to each of the battles in politics, media and academia.

In politics, the most vulnerable area to the invasion of the Warm-Blooded Army is the middle. A warm-blooded strategist, therefore, must plan the attack accordingly. This means that he or she must target the Independents, Reformists, moderates, liberal conservatives, conservative liberals and swing voters first. Once the Warm-Blooded Army achieves reasonable success in the middle, the strategist can move more troops to invade the right and left wing territories of the political battlefield that are dominated by strict conservatives and liberals.

In academia, too, it will be easier to look for support for bio-economic engineering among professors of sciences and engineering rather than among professors of economics and social sciences. A warm-blooded strategist, therefore, should plan for more results along the frontier of natural sciences than the frontier of social sciences.

Along the three frontiers of politics, media and academia, a warm-blooded strategist should expect quick and solid victories in the first two frontiers. Final, solid victory in the frontier of academia is much harder to obtain. Victory in the frontiers of politics and media requires only persuading the people to seek warm-blooded solutions in economics and politics. Solid victory in academia requires much more than just convincing the professors by the warm-blooded message. It requires building the foundation of the new discipline of bio-economic engineering. While this is feasible, it just requires some time. It will take at least eight years for this new discipline to mature and be used as a weapon of mass destruction in the war against reptilism.

Tactics of the First Battle

Since the war will involve fighting along the three frontiers of politics, media and academia, tactics too will involve three types: *political tactics, media tactics* and *academia tactics*.

Tactics along these three frontiers should be designed to pursue the objective of *incremental attrition*—attrition of the reptilian enemy's fighters, intellectual weapons and staying power. At a certain point during the third battle, it will be time to *strike heavily and viciously* with the emphasis placed on complete destruction of the reptilian enemy's will to continue to fight.

Political Tactics

The most important tactic in the first battle is to announce the birth of a Warm-Blooded Version of the *Reform Party*. We need to have a special celebration for this occasion and use the opportunity to expose warm-blooded economics and politics to more publicity.

The official date for the birth of the Warm-Blooded Reform Party will be a memorable date all future generations will celebrate every year. After all, this represents a major leap for all Reformists and Independents from being mammal-like reptiles of our political system to being true mammals!

Following this leap, the next political tactic is to increase the number of supporters of the Warm-Blooded Reform Party continuously. To do so, warm-blooded tacticians must act like the marketing and publicity staff of big companies trying to win customers for their products. The customers are ordinary people. They need products in economics and politics. They must buy something. At present, there are only two products: reptilian cold-bloodedness offered by the Republican Party and reptilian hibernation offered by the Democratic Party. The Warm-Blooded Reform Party will offer a new superior product: the first warm-blooded mammalian version in economics and politics in history!

Offering superior products is not enough for companies to persuade customers to buy them. Companies must have a good marketing strategy. Likewise, offering superior products in economics and politics will not be enough to win the politics frontier. The Warm-Blooded Army must have a good marketing and publicity strategy.

Warm-blooded tacticians must advertise the new warm-blooded products to ordinary people. We need to use marketing tactics that successful companies use to promote their products. These tactics will try to attract the attention of customers in politics and economics to make them aware of the availability of warm-blooded mammalian products. To achieve this, the warm-blooded fighters will be encouraged to display their ranks in the army, especially if the rank is sergeant and above. They may decide to wear their uniforms occasionally, like members of the Salvation Army. The Warm-Blooded Army will not stick to a fixed type of uniform. There will be several of them to satisfy the different tastes of different fighters.

Another form of political advertising is bumper stickers that promote warm-bloodedness and denounce reptilism. The fighters will encourage people to flood politicians, key economists, chairman and governors of the Federal Reserve Board with letters reminding them that the Dark Age of Reptilian Economics and Politics is coming to an end soon. If politicians and economists fail to adjust to the new age, they will face the fate of dinosaurs!

To sell uniforms of the Warm-Blooded Army, bumper stickers, cards, souvenirs and other gifts that promote the message of warm-bloodedness, we will need to open the *Warm-Blooded Store*. During the first battle, the Warm-Blooded Store will start as a mail order catalog store. As the message of warm-bloodedness attracts more people in the subsequent battles, the Warm-Blooded store will expand by opening new branches in several selected malls.

In designing marketing items for advertising the message of warm-bloodedness, we must think about how to influence and drive the political-psychological discontent. We need to crystallize the discontent among people in general and their concerns about economics and politics in particular. Then, we can organize the discontented and militarize them with intellectual weapons to fight reptilism. This dynamic process will be supported by small incremental victories in the frontier of politics, media and academia. This process, in turn, will provide the Warm-Blooded Army with increasing quantities of recruits and supplies. It is these kinds of cellular maneuvers that will exhaust the reptilian enemies.

A key psychological factor for increasing discontent is how to treat those who surrender in the war against reptilism. We will encounter many enemy individuals who decide to throw down their intellectual weapons and surrender to the Warm-Blooded Army. In conventional wars, there are minimum standards for the treatment of those who surrender. The rules set for the intellectual war against reptilism must be more civilized and more humanitarian than the rules for conventional wars. This means that all the surrendered enemy troops should be treated with humanity and dignity. The level of treatment, however, will depend on the way they surrender.

Some enemies will surrender with extreme humiliation as they confess that they have been fooled by cold-blooded conservatism or hibernating liberalism! The warm-blooded troops must recognize a simple rule: the more humiliating the words of those who surrender, the higher the level of courtesy and honor they will receive! In fact, any person who surrenders is no longer an enemy or a prisoner of the intellectual war, even if he or she was a Republican or a Democrat running for presidency, Congress or Senate! We must give those persons an opportunity to join the Warm-Blooded Army and the Warm-Blooded Reform Party. We must let them run as dignified Warm-Blooded candidates even if they come to us at the last minute before the election day. Unlike conventional war where prisoners are not trusted, the war against reptilism will be different. We must trust those who surrender as if they never have fought against the Warm-Blooded Army!

An effective tactic is to offer an *honorary* award for the most *humiliating* confession! To increase the chance of winning, the confessions should be taped during the highest emotional peak. These tapes will be played over and over again to customers in politics and economics. The humiliating confessions will turn off those who buy reptilian products in economics and politics. Once more customers are turned off by reptilism, they will be more open to warm-blooded alternatives and be curious to try them.

To increase the effectiveness of this tactic, Warm-Blooded Books will launch a joint effort with the Warm-Blooded Army to publish the most humiliating confessions in a book titled *"Heartbreaking Confessions: How Do Mammalian Reformists Feel about Their Reptilian Roots?"*

Media Tactics

Before the great expansion of the modern media, people relied on communicating their ideas and beliefs by talking face to face. As the media expands more and more, people spend less time talking to each other and more time listening to the media. Such a trend reduces the influence of word of mouth and increases the role of the media.

At present, all the media channels talk only about reptilian options in economics and politics. They haven't yet recognized the middle where warm-blooded mammalian species in economics and politics will evolve. This means that the Warm-

Blooded Army may not have a big influence in media channels at the beginning of the first battle.

The lack of fair access to media channels during the early phase of the war will hurt the destructive capability of the Warm-Blooded Army. Progress in invading more territories of the reptilian enemies will be slower than most warm-blooded fighters would like to see. The fighters should not dwell on the weakness that a lack of fair access to media channels produces. Instead, they should make maximum use of what they have to reach people; they still can deliver their messages by words of mouth. That was exactly what people were doing before the expansion of media. Maybe it is time for people to talk more to each other and listen less to the media.

But if we rely more on personal talks to people during the first battle it does not mean we give up on the media. The Warm-Blooded Army must fight persistently to have the access it deserves in the media. To gain such access, tacticians in the army will use two tactics: 1) *persuasion tactics*, and 2) *offensive tactics*.

The persuasion tactics—as the word implies—will try to peacefully persuade the executives of the media channels that it is in their financial interest to let the fighters of the Warm-Blooded Army have fair access in their channels. People are encouraged to write to the media channels they favor. They should explain to the media executives that they would serve the audience more effectively if they open their doors to warm-blooded economics and politics. This should be done in a friendly and polite manner.

The persuasion tactic is just a peaceful warning to push the media into recognizing warm-blooded economics and politics without ugly, brutal fighting. It would not be wise, however, to rely on warnings only. They must be accompanied by offensive tactics.

The offensive tactics will try to steal the audience from current media channels by opening new channels dedicated to warm-bloodedness. This will result in reduced audiences and a drop in revenue for typical channels. The executives will panic as the revenue falls, and they will take the earlier warnings about opening their doors to warm-bloodedness more seriously.

The new channels dedicated to warm-bloodedness will include: 1) a new monthly magazine called *Warm-Blooded Thinking* that will attract authors and an audience interested to fight using articles instead of books; 2) a new radio station called the *Warm-Blooded Voice* that will offer a mammalian voice clearly distinguished from the reptilian voices heard in other conservative and liberal stations; and 3) a new TV channel called the *Warm-Blooded Channel* that will feature educational, entertaining and humorous programs covering similarities between biology and economics/politics. While these warm-blooded media channels will likely reach out and touch their audience during the second and third battles, the threat of using these media channels may be used as an effective tactic during the first battle.

Academia Tactics

After some encouraging progress along the frontiers of politics and media, it will be time to deploy troops to fight at the academia frontier. To succeed there, we need to raise large funds to support more research and developments in the new discipline of bio-economic engineering. We must recognize the professors and researchers as high-tech defense contractors working hard and smart to support the mass destruction capability of the Warm-Blooded Army. They will provide crucial service in the war against reptilism. In return, they must be paid well.

To maximize funds raised for academic research, the warm-blooded fighters should inform people that whatever they contribute is not just charity to help the cause of warm-bloodedness in economics and politics. It is a wise investment in the future of our nation and the future of our children. Warm-bloodedness will have the potential of bringing trillions of dollars as a result of eliminating business cycles, operating the economy at stabilized, vigorous levels, and opening and balancing trade! The amount we and our children receive will depend on the advancement we achieve in the frontier of academia. The more money we pump in and the more incentives the professors and researchers receive, the more the level of warm-bloodedness in economics and politics our children will enjoy. It is very possible that whatever we raise will provide a several thousandfold return in future benefits for our children. There is no other investment in the world that comes close—even a portfolio of the most attractive Nasdaq stocks.

In addition to raising funds for academic research to support warm-bloodedness in economics and politics, it will be helpful to use an additional tactic of offering contests and awards for the best academic achievements in bio-economic engineering.

Despite its huge potential, the academia frontier will still be the most difficult one to win! The warm-blooded fighters should not expect to achieve a lot, in general, during the first battle of the year 2000. Things will be slow and will take some time. But once this frontier gains momentum, it will be impossible to stop it. Both findings and funding will increase drastically. When the frontier of academia achieves good progress, we will know that the war against reptilism is almost over. This is likely to happen at the third, and hopefully last battle, ending at the historical year 2008 that will mark the beginning of the new warm-blooded era in human history.

15

The Midst of Economic/Political Armageddon

We Stand at Armageddon and we battle for the Lord.

President Theodore Roosevelt
Speech at Progressive Party Convention,
Chicago, June 17, 1912

The Final Great Battle between Good and Evil

As we come close to the end of this book, it is time to say "*good-bye*." I hope I have succeeded in explaining to you the current reptilian reality either in its cold-blooded conservative form, its hibernating liberal form or any mix of the two. I also hope that you will be convinced that warm-bloodedness in economics and politics is possible if we put our mind on it and try hard and act smart.

Most important, I hope you will be prepared for the *economic and political version of Armageddon, the intellectual and cultural World War* that will start first in the U.S. during the year 2000 and then spread to all countries around the globe. Like the biblical Armageddon, the Economic/Political Armageddon will involve two irreconcilable armies fighting fiercely: 1) the *satanic army* representing reptilism in economics and politics in both conservative and liberal forms and 2) the *good army* representing warm-bloodedness and mammalism. The satanic Reptilian Army currently occupies and rules the entire world of economics and politics, and the Warm-Blooded Army will have to declare war against it and fight to deliver humans from its evils.

In addition to this similarity in featuring a battle between good and evil, the coming economic/political Armageddon will be similar to the movie *Armageddon* in which a gigantic asteroid was about to crash into the Earth. Like the movie, the first pieces of the economic/political asteroid will not be as gigantic and catastrophic as the ones that will follow. This early warning serves a good purpose. It lets the people be prepared for the big event. It also motivates them to make maximum use of the little, precious time left.

The first two pieces of the economic/political asteroid will hit Earth with the announcement of the Warm-Blooded Army and the Warm-Blooded Version of the Reform Party. Following this event, many warm-blooded fighters will intellectually bombard the planet with more asteroid pieces. But, the most gigantic one will hit on the election year 2008 when the first warm-blooded President and first warm-blooded houses of Congress win the trust of the American people. This final asteroid crash will cause a *Deep Impact* and a *Tidal Wave* of new economic and political culture and spirit, a wave hundreds of feet high spreading and covering all the world!

Following the Deep Impact and Tidal Wave, all the current reptilian economic and political systems in all nations will be drowned and utterly destroyed! The list will include capitalism, socialism, communism and everything in between! Despite this destructive side, the Deep Impact and Tidal Wave will have their creative sides as well. They will mark the *end of the evil dominance of reptilism* in the world of economics and politics and *the beginning of the new kingdom of warm-bloodedness and mammalism,* a kingdom that will last from the dawn of the new millennium until the end of time.

Your Role in Economic/Political Armageddon

With the coming Economic/Political Armageddon and Deep Impact, the first decade of the new millennium will be indeed a very special time in history. And you have the privilege to witness this time, something all your ancestors never had and all your descendants will envy you for having. So you need to do your homework to make use of this precious opportunity. You must take a position right now on what side you would like to be in the coming Economic/Political Armageddon and Deep Impact.

Regardless of what you choose, you must live with the consequences of your choice for the rest of your life. One day you will have to answer many tough questions your children and grandchildren will ask: What did you do during the Economic/ Political Armageddon? Were you fighting for good or for evil? Were you on the side of warm-bloodedness or reptilism? Were you trapped in the reptilian Republican and Democratic Parties or did you flee to the Warm-Blooded Reform Party? Was the beginning of the new millennium a time of glory or a time of disgrace to you and your descendants?

I hope it will be a time of glory and that you choose the side of warm-bloodedness and mammalism rather than cold-bloodedness, hibernation and reptilism. If you choose so, you should join the Warm-Blooded Reform Party. You should also consider joining the Warm-Blooded Army in either its technical or fighting troops, and contributing to achieve its mission to defeat the evil forces of reptilism.

If you decide to join the Warm-Blooded Army, I sincerely welcome you. I would like to remind those who decide to join the army that our fight against the reptilian economic and political species is intellectual, not physical. We will never tolerate any violence in the coming Economic/Political Armageddon. We have to achieve our means peacefully and through the democratic process, following the successful examples of Mahatma Gandhi and Martin Luther King. And we, too, will eventually win. Every fighter must fight intellectually according to the highest moral and ethical standards. Any person who is involved in violence or breaks any law will be expelled immediately from the Warm-

Blooded Army and will never recover membership. There will be no excuse.

What Will the Second Volumes of This Book Series Offer in the Coming Armageddon?

Before I finally say "good-bye," I would like to mention that I will have an opportunity to meet with you again in my second volume of this series. It will be titled *"The Second Age of Reptiles: Volume II: Striking   Discoveries about the History of Economic and Political Species,"* and will be published in the presidential election year 2004.

The second volume will answer a logical question that some readers may already have asked: "If we live in the Age of Reptilian Economics and Politics, then what are the other ages in human history?" Well, there are five ages in life history that include the ages of 1) invertebrates, 2) fish, 3) amphibians, 4) reptiles and 5) mammals. Interestingly, there are also five similar ages in human history! They include 1) Prehistoric Ages, 2) Ancient Ages, 3) Middle Ages, 4) what we falsely call "Modern Ages," and 5) Ages of Warm-Blooded Mammalian Economics and Politics coming soon. Thus human history mirrors life history in number of ages, development patterns and direction! This is a new, revolutionary theory proposing that human history has meaning and definite direction, which is in contrast with the current accepted view among most historians that history is random and has no meaning!

You will see in the second volume overwhelming evidence showing that each of the first four ages of human history *fits nicely* with its corresponding age of life history like pieces of a *jigsaw puzzle!* The puzzle solution is not complete yet, as humans have not entered *The Age of Mammalian Economics and Politics.* Once they enter that age, the fifth piece will fit nicely as well, thus completing the final solution of the challenging puzzle of human history!

As you read the second volume, you will have fun playing an interesting jigsaw puzzle game and connecting the numerous pieces of human history to those of life history to come up with a final, meaningful picture. Playing this game, however, will not be just only for fun, entertainment or having a good time. It will be a serious business as well, helping us *explore* the *meaning of the past*, the *direction of the present*, and the *destiny of the future*!

I hope that the order of this book series is logical. This volume has focused on the *Radical Discoveries about* the *Nature of Species in the World of Economics and Politics*. After we've understood the nature of species, it is time to look at their *history* since nature and history complement each other. The second volume will also complement this one in another way. This volume promotes the new discipline of bio-economic engineering that comes from crossbreeding economics and biology. Similarly, the second volume will promote *bio-historical engineering*—another new, fascinating discipline that will evolve from crossbreeding paleontology (the science of life history) and human history!

In addition, the second volume will explore more war tactics and how we can use the combination of bio-economic engineering and bio-historical engineering as intellectual weapons of mass destruction against the reptilian economic and political species. These weapons will be needed during the presidential election year 2004. Also, we will announce, around the publication date, the *tenth technical troop* of the Warm-Blooded Army. That troop will include paleontologists and historians teaming up together as *bio-historical engineers*, and looking forward to exploring exciting intellectual adventures!

Finally, I hope my second volume will inspire bio-historical engineers in their adventures and help them exterminate the reptilian enemies, both cold-blooded conservatives and hibernating liberal, at a faster rate during the following election years. I also hope that as you read my second volume and subsequent ones, you will be convinced more and more that we together can bring an end to the *Dark Age of Reptilian Economics and Politics*, and usher in the beginning of the *Enlightened Age of Mammalian Economics and Politics*.

Notes and Bibliography

Introductory Quotation

1. Lawrence Malkin, *The National Debt*, Mentor Book, 1987, p. 215.

Chapter 1: Cold-Bloodedness and Its Misery

1. P.J. O'Rourke, *Republican Party Reptile: The Confessions, Adventures, Essays, and Outrages of P.J. O'Rourke*, Morgan Entrekin Book, The Atlantic Monthly Press, New York, 1987, p. xv.
2. Paul A Samuelson and William D. Nordhaus, *Economics*, Thirteenth edition, McGraw-Hill Book Company, 1989, p. 212.
3. Ibid, p. 204.
4. M. Harvey Brenner, *Influence of Social Environment on Psychopathology: The Historical Perspective*, in James E. Barrett et al. (eds.), *Stress and Mental Disorder*, Raven Press, New York, 1979, pp. 8-24.
5. A.W. Phillips, *"The Relationship between Unemployment and the Rate of Change of Money Wages in the United Kingdom, 1861-1957,"* *Economica* 25, November 1958, pp. 283-299.

Chapter 4: Messengers Living the Messages

1. Todd G. Buchholz, *New Ideas from Dead Economists*, Plume Book, 1990, p. 3.

2. *"Speed, Simplicity and Self-Confidence"* was one of the corporate slogans of the General Electric Company throughout the early 1990s.

Chapter 5: Messengers Living the Messages

1. Todd G. Buchholz, *New Ideas from Dead Economists*, Plume Book, 1990, p. 12.
2. Ibid., p. 121.
3. John Maynard Keynes, *The Collected Writings of John Maynard Keynes*, London: Macmillan/St. Martin's Press for the Royal Economic Society, 1973, Vol. VII, pp. 380-381.
4. Paul Samuelson, *Lord Keynes and the General Theory, Econometrica*, vol. 14 (1946), p. 190.
5. Paul Krugman, *Peddling Prosperity: Economic Sense and Nonsense in the Age of Diminished Expectations*, W.W. Norton & Company, 1994, p. 33.
6. William Greider, *Secrets of the Temple*, Simon & Schuster: Touchstone, 1989, p. 318.

Chapter 6: The Cold-Blooded Species

1. Milton & Rose Friedman, *Free to Choose: A Personal Statement*, Harvest/HBJ Book, New York, p. 39.

Chapter 9: Abandoning Reptilism and Seeking Warm-Bloodedness

1. Martin & Susan Tolchin, *Buying into America*, Berkeley Books, New York, 1989, p. 255
2. Ravi Batra, *The Myth of Free Trade*, Simon & Schuster Touchstone Book, 1993, p. 231.

Chapter 13: Declaring War

1. Paul Krugman, *Peddling Prosperity: Economic Sense and Nonsense in the Age of Diminished Expectations*, W.W. Norton & Company, 1994, p. 292.

Index

About the Author

Raafat Kammel is a the founder of *Kammelosaur Warm-blooded Research Inc*, a new firm that explores and markets business opportunities arising from this book series and from the coming warm-blooded mammalian evolution of economics and politics.

The three words comprising the author's firm—*Kammelosaur Warm-blooded Research*—summarize three objectives that complement those of the book series. The first objective is to persuade every responsible citizen to have the suffix "*osaur*" added to his or her family name in order to match the reptilian reality in economics and politics. After all, we live in the *Second Age of Reptiles*. The second objective is to start changing the ugly reality by proclaiming *warm-blooded* economics and politics as a natural right for all humans. The third objective is to identify continuous *research* in bridging natural and social sciences as the mean to reach the warm-blooded status soon.

Kammel's background is unique. During his diversified professional career, he worked on computer modeling of financial markets and Wall Street. This experience introduced him to economics. As he became attracted to the field, he could not stop himself from spending twelve years studying economics and another related subject: biology. This was twice as long as it took him to finish his BS and MS degrees in engineering. With close to twenty years of in-depth studies and research in economics, biology and engineering, Kammel has developed a rare perspective that perhaps no author or thinker in the entire world has tried to acquire. He has mastered the skills to blend knowledge from economics, biology and engineering in creative, artistic and humorous ways.

Kammel received his BS in aeronautical engineering from Cairo University and his MS in mechanical engineering from University of Toronto. He is married and lives with his wife and two children in Peabody, Massachusetts.